Boards That Work

A Practical Guide to Building Effective Association Boards

Douglas C. Eadie

Edited by Linda Daily
Cover and interior design by Design Consultants

Cover illustration: Charles Biederman, *New York, February 1936*, 1936
Gouache on composition board
Sheet: 29 15/16 x 21 3/16 in (76 x 53.8 cm.)
Collection of Whitney Museum of American Art
Purchase, with funds from the Drawing Committee
85.57

American Society of Association Executives
1575 Eye Street, N.W.
Washington, DC 20005-1168

Printed in the United States

ISBN 0-88034-091-6

Library of Congress Cataloging-in-Publication Data

Eadie, Douglas C.
    Boards that work: a practical guide to building effective association boards/Douglas C. Eadie
        p. cm.
    ISBN 0-88034-091-6
    1. Associations, institutions, etc.—Management. 2. Nonprofit organizations—Management. 3.
    Directors of corporations.
I. American Society of Association Executives. II. Title. III. Title: Association boards.
HV41.E18 1994   94-44298
060'.68'4—dc20   CIP

Contents

SECTION I: BEYOND INHERITANCE TO DESIGN

SECTION II: ORGANIZING THE BOARD

SECTION III: DOING GOVERNANCE WORK

SECTION IV: RETREATS, CHANGE MANAGEMENT, AND SOURCES

To My Parents,
Ina Mae and William Clay Eadie

Acknowledgments

Despite the traditional neglect of board leadership as a subject, over the past decade a number of pioneers have done path-breaking work on governance that has enriched and inspired the preparation of this book, even as our ideas have occasionally diverged. Most notable are Peter Drucker, whose early attention to nonprofit management helped to clarify the appropriate role of the nonprofit board; Cyril Houle, whose *Governing Boards* is an indispensable starting point and comprehensive primer for anyone interested in board leadership; and John Carver, whose *Boards That Make a Difference* makes a compelling case for treating boards as a serious business and examines in-depth the policy formulation process as the preeminent vehicle for the exercise of board leadership.

A major resource on governance is the National Center for Nonprofit Boards, which has significantly advanced the field over the past decade through the publication of several useful monographs touching on virtually every facet of board leadership. The American Society of Association Executives has also contributed to the body of knowledge on board leadership through articles in its two periodicals—*Association Management* and *Leadership Magazine*—and various books.

In the field of strategy, I am indebted to Professor Nathan D. Grundstein, Professor Emeritus of Management Policy, at the Weatherhead School of Case Western Reserve University. His teaching and writing have enriched my understanding of strategic thinking. Little concerned with the mechanics of planning, Professor Grundstein has explored in a three-volume series the fundamental underpinnings of the strategic logic, thereby laying the foundation for more powerful applications in the nonprofit sector.

But theory has less to do with this book than experience. In this regard I owe the deepest gratitude to the hundreds of nonprofit boards, chief executive officers, and executive teams with whom I have worked over the past two decades, including several associations. The wisdom in this book comes from their practical experience, and the lessons that I share were learned in working with them. In a very real sense, these clients are my partners and coauthors and deserve a large measure of credit for whatever virtues this book possesses.

I want to express my appreciation to ASAE's Karen Loper and Anna Nunan, without whose advice and encouragement my writing job would have been much more difficult. I owe a debt of gratitude to my wife, Barbara Krai Eadie—colleague, friend, and confidante—for her faith in my capabilities, her steadfast support, and her unfailingly wise counsel from first to last page. And, finally, I want to thank my children, Jennifer and William, whose love and companionship inspired and energized me throughout the writing of this book.

Douglas C. Eadie
Cleveland, Ohio
December 1994

Chapter One
Overview

A Matter of Much Importance

Effective boards do make a difference to associations. When we see a fundamentally healthy association that is expanding its capabilities and diversifying its services, revenues, and membership, we can safely assume that an effective board is at work, in close alliance with a strong chief executive officer. And the odds are that this thriving association is tapping fully the experience, talent, expertise, and networks that volunteers bring to the board room. By contrast, when we come across an organization that appears adrift, lacking strategic focus and a clear sense of mission, we are more likely than not witnessing the impact of ineffective board leadership. Most of us have learned from experience that executive management—no matter how capable—and planning and management systems—no matter how sophisticated—cannot alone carry the full burden of leading an association. Long-term association success depends on strong board leadership as well.

Governing Boards

What is a nonprofit association board? Cyril Houle has supplied us with a practical general definition of a board as "an organized group of people with the authority collectively to control and foster an institution that is usually administered by a qualified executive and staff." This book is about nonprofit association *governing* boards, which John Carver has described as "the board of ultimate corporate accountability."

The governing board is always positioned at the top of the organization. 'Corporate board,' 'board of directors,' 'board of trustees,' 'board of regents,' and similar titles denote groups that have authority exceeded only by owners and the state. The governing board is as high in the structure as one can go and still be within the organizational framework. Its total authority is matched by its total accountability for all corporate activity.

The Board-Chief Executive Alliance

This book is intended for both partners comprising an association's top leadership team: the board and its chief executive officer. Consisting of part-time volunteers, association boards cannot hope to govern effectively without the strong support of, and creative collaboration with, the chief executive. On the other hand, sustained, strong, chief executive leadership depends on a positive and productive working partnership with the board.

Building and maintaining this close working partnership is a survival matter for association chief executives, who typically bear the brunt of the blame when boards become frustrated with their performance and when the ties that bind the two partners fray. Indeed, there is good reason to believe that the declining tenure of association chief executives has more to do with eroding board-chief executive relationships than any other factor.

Traditional Neglect

Surprisingly, in light of the obvious importance of effective boards to the success of nonprofit organizations generally, and to associations and their chief executives in particular, the subject of board capability building has received relatively little attention until recently. Little thought was given to the bottom-line contribution that boards can make to their organizations, to the leadership roles that boards can play, and to the structure and process that support boards in carrying out their leadership roles. At best, boards were an interesting tributary outside of mainstream leadership and management concerns. More attention was paid to keeping them from doing damage (usually in the form of "dabbling" in administrative matters) than to realizing their leadership potential.

Unfortunately, the traditional "little golden rules" that have so often been taught in board training programs have tended to be untested conventional wisdom that is just as apt to cause harm as produce benefits in practice. For example, how often have we heard that smaller boards are better and larger boards unwieldy, even though board size should be a direct function of the needs and capabilities of particular associations? Or what about the oft-taught maxim that finished staff work is a virtue when dealing with boards? In practice, truly finished work can leave a board with little to do but thumb through a tome it has not influenced and will most likely not embrace as its own.

Change in the Nonprofit World

This is a time of exciting change in the world of nonprofit leadership and management. The significant progress being made in the following five areas promises to transform nonprofit management in the near-term future, and this book draws on the advances being made:

- **Governance**—A new leadership model is emerging that sees the nonprofit board as a positive, proactive contributor to organizational leadership, rather than as an audience reacting to finished staff work.

- **Chief Executive Leadership**—We now realize that the chief executive in today's world must be much more than the traditional boss. Far more important than merely commanding are creative organizational design and the facilitation of an organization's work, including the responsibility to assist the board in developing its leadership capability.

- **Strategy**—Going well beyond traditional long-range planning, with its pounds of paper and projections of the present into an unknown future, the more contemporary strategic management process is highly selective and focused on both organizational change and concrete action.

- **Human Resource Development**—Work in psychology and organizational behavior has opened new doors in understanding how people learn and has provided us with practical tools for developing individual potential. Since organizations are above all else people, helping individuals to grow and to realize their promise more fully is a powerful organizational development tool.

- **Change Management**—We now have practical tools to ensure that planned change actually takes place, rather than being overwhelmed by the pressures and crises of every-day association life. Boards committed to developing their leadership capability can move forward knowing that their investment of time and energy will yield a return.

This Book's Intent

The basic purpose of this book is to provide association board members, chief executive officers, and managers with practical guidance in *designing* and *managing* their association *board business*. The key assumption that has guided my writing is that *boards of directors are one of the most important businesses or programs of any association and that the effectiveness of boards depends on their being consciously designed and meticulously managed.*

Two additional assumptions are at the heart of this book:

- Effective association leadership involves a creative, dynamic partnership among the board, chief executive, and staff; the boundaries that separate the work of each partner are inevitably fuzzy, and the division of labor will change over time as the association and its environment evolve.

- Effective boards must develop their own capability, with the assistance of the chief executive and staff; merely telling a board how to be effective, no matter how elaborate the training exercise, is unlikely to produce significant change.

Not a Cookbook

Practical guidance does not mean the production of a board "cookbook" that provides simple, straightforward answers to every question. To take full advantage of the advice and counsel in the pages that follow, association boards and their chief executive officers must translate broad guidelines into specific practice. They must tailor and elaborate the answers to match their associations' unique histories and traditions, their unique cultures and political dynamics, and their unique needs and capabilities. Every association is unique, and there are truly no all-purpose prescriptions for building association boards.

The business of strengthening association board leadership is by its very nature positive and creative. In essence, it involves unleashing tremendous human potential in the service of both the ends of the association and the needs of the volunteers serving on the board. Americans need and want to contribute, and strong boards provide them with one of the most important opportunities to do so. This creative leadership development process has less to do with rules, discipline, and control than with openness, curiosity, flexibility, and a commitment to innovation.

In the Following Pages

A key focus of this book is what I call *board leadership design*. This process basically involves an association board's deciding what kind of governing body it wants to be and what it wants to accomplish, and then devising practical ways to accomplish this "governance mission." I pay considerable attention to those association leadership functions that offer boards the greatest opportunity to capitalize fully on their resources, to exercise significant influence on association affairs, and to produce substantial positive impact. Chief among these are strategic and operational planning, budget preparation, performance monitoring, and external relations. I also deal with other important board design issues: board membership and structure, the board-executive partnership, how to utilize retreats as a board-development vehicle, and how to ensure that planned board capability-building initiatives are actually implemented.

This book does not attempt to cover every aspect of nonprofit association board structure and process, or merely to restate what others have said. Rather, its intent is to add value by addressing facets of board leadership not heretofore fully explored. The reader can turn to Cyril Houle's *Governing Boards* for a comprehensive description of board operations and to the various monographs published by the National Center for Nonprofit Boards for specific information on a number of governance subjects.

The chapters that follow are basically intended to be modular, allowing the reader to sample any one or more that may be of particular interest, rather than being forced to proceed through the chapters in order. However, there is a logical flow, and reading the following chapters in sequence will facilitate understanding of a complex subject.

- Chapter 2 explores the tremendous potential contribution that boards can make to their associations and examines why this potential is often unrealized.

- Chapter 3 describes a practical, tested process of *designing* boards, in terms of their leadership missions, membership, leadership processes, and structures.

- Chapter 4 describes the key elements of an association board's leadership mission.

- Chapter 5 discusses ways to strengthen board membership, through more systematic approaches to identifying desired attributes and qualifications, and to identifying and selecting candidates.

- Chapter 6 focuses on two of the most important ways to enhance board effectiveness: by implementing a formal board performance management process and enhancing board members' leadership skills.

- Chapter 7 addresses a number of structural issues, including how broad functional committees can serve as powerful vehicles for board leadership, if they are well designed, led, and supported; the role of the board chair, and how to untangle governance from other kinds of volunteering.

- Chapter 8 looks at the subject of the board-executive partnership, suggesting practical ways to build positive, productive relationships that serve association interests.

- Chapter 9 provides detailed guidance for involving boards in the strategic and operational planning processes in a creative, proactive fashion that fully taps the board as a precious resource to the association.

- Chapter 10 describes how the board can carry out its performance oversight responsibilities without getting embroiled in trivial detail or snowed by reams of paper and dog 'n pony briefings.

- Chapter 11 explores creative ways boards can strengthen their associations' image, public relations, and relationships with key stakeholder organizations.

- Chapter 12 offers practical tips for putting together retreats that can facilitate the exercise of strong board leadership.

- Chapter 13 arms the reader with detailed guidance for managing the changes that are normally required to implement a new board leadership design.

- Chapter 14 describes sources to which the reader might go for inspiration and further information on board leadership, strategic planning, change management, and human growth and development.

Beyond Inheritance to Design

Chapter Two
Bright Promise

The Stakes Are High

Associations belong to a huge, amazingly diverse, and rapidly growing nonprofit sector in the United States. National and state professional and trade associations, universities and colleges, churches, hospitals, neighborhood development corporations, social service agencies, organizations to aid the homeless and the hungry, shelters for abused women, social and service clubs, civic associations—these are but a few examples from a list that goes on and on. It has been estimated that some 1.2 million private, nonprofit organizations are operating in the United States, including an estimated 100,000 or more associations. Every nonprofit organization in the country is governed by a board of directors, which means that millions of nonprofit board seats must be filled by volunteers.

No one questions the importance of the nonprofit sector in today's world. To Peter Drucker, nonprofit organizations are "central to American society and are indeed its most distinguishing feature." The phenomenal growth of nonprofit organizations is probably in large measure due to their flexibility. Nonprofits can focus on specific purposes free of the political and bureaucratic constraints of government and untrammeled by the profit requirement of business. And nonprofit boards have become a powerful vehicle for government-business cooperation in addressing issues that neither can as effectively tackle alone.

A large and influential segment of the nonprofit sector, the thousands of local, state, regional, and national associations do immense social and economic good in the United States, and the value of their contribution to the country's advancement must amount to billions of dollars annually. Because of associations, national direction setting and policy formulation are better informed, corporate and individual members receive information and technical assistance critical to their success, professional standards are upgraded, and new technologies are effectively disseminated. Without a doubt, building strong, effective associations is a matter of critical national importance.

The Board Contribution

We can measure association effectiveness in a number of ways—steady movement toward realizing a clear vision, demonstrated progress in carrying out mission and goals, membership satisfaction, growth in membership and revenues, to name some of the more obvious measures. And who would disagree that one of the major contributors to an association's success is its board of directors? The minimalist view of nonprofit association boards, as basically aloof policy-making vehicles, does not begin to capture the tremendous potential of association boards. In concert with chief executives and with the support of planning and management systems, they can play a creative and powerful role in:

- Fashioning an association's strategic framework: its values, vision for the future, mission, and broad goals
- Establishing key performance targets
- Formulating policies to govern association practices
- Ensuring the membership that the association is performing effectively and efficiently
- Bringing knowledge, experience, talent, and expertise to association affairs
- Putting board members' ties to political and financial resources to work for their associations

Opportunities for Volunteers

We should keep in mind that association boards not only can contribute powerfully to the welfare of the associations that they have been established to govern, they can also serve as one of the most valuable vehicles for meaningful volunteer involvement in associations. Volunteering time is a great American tradition that results from a strong need to "pay back" that cannot be entirely satisfied by opening one's checkbook. Association boards can provide a unique opportunity to serve while also satisfying less altruistic needs, such as satisfaction, professional growth, networking, and recognition.

Satisfaction

Volunteers on boards can experience the intense satisfaction that comes from having a powerful impact on organizations they care about. Because of their efforts as board members, programs and services are enhanced, revenues are strengthened, productivity is improved, and membership increases. Volunteers serving on strong boards know that they make a difference and that the investment of their time and energy yields a handsome return.

Professional Growth

Volunteers serving on boards can also grow in knowledge, wisdom, and professional and executive skills as a result of their participation in the governance process. Effective boards involve their members at a high level in such demanding areas as strategic planning, policy formulation, performance monitoring, and chief executive evaluation. Kicking back her feet in the evening, after a long Saturday spent at the annual strategic retreat, an association board member knows that her brain has been stretched in fashioning her association's vision, clarifying its mission, and setting its long-range directions. To her surprise, she is armed with a number of ideas about applying strategic planning techniques that she wants to test back at her own shop. And the half-day just spent with her association board's executive committee, closeted with their new chief executive officer—comparing her performance over the past year to the objectives that were set earlier in the year—has taught her a lot she didn't know about the nature of the executive task and about human interaction and communication. No question about it: Governing can be a potent growth hormone.

Networking

Of course, association board service can also expand a volunteer's professional and personal networks. Not surprisingly, the average board member is apt to be an accomplished, intellectually curious, and ambitious person with a keen interest in the people around her. It is difficult to imagine a more promising environment for extending one's network.

Recognition

An association volunteer can achieve public recognition through board service, thereby earning the ego satisfaction that most of us, our protestations notwithstanding, naturally crave. As a member of his or her association board, she may see herself quoted in the morning newspaper, he may find himself participating in a television talk show, or on the platform at a civic forum he is about to keynote.

Not Pie-in-the-Sky

These are not pie-in-the-sky expectations. Accomplished people interested in volunteering their time should take a good hard look at association board service as a splendid opportunity to meet important social and personal needs. What better way to profoundly influence an association's directions and to produce significant social good than to participate in its governance, fashioning its strategies and setting its policies? What better place to meet accomplished individuals from diverse backgrounds with varied perspectives who have much to teach than on a board? And what better place to put one's capabilities to the fullest test than in doing the challenging, technically complex, and patently important work of a governance board?

But in the Real World

The good news is that boards of directors can make a powerful contribution to association leadership while providing an experience for board members that is personally and professionally rewarding. The bad news is that effective association boards capable of generating such impressive outcomes are the product of hard labor and may be the distinct exception to the rule. Be forewarned that the gap between good intentions and bright promise on the one hand, and reality, on the other, can be depressingly wide. Nonprofit association boards are frequently ineffectual—reacting rather than leading, rubber-stamping rather than directing, enervating rather than energizing their members—providing a boring rather than a challenging experience.

An association member venturing into the governance terrain is, sad to say, just as likely to suffer the disappointment of dashed expectations as to experience the high of grappling successfully with the truly big questions. To be sure, there are effective nonprofit association boards with actively engaged, fully contributing members; but they are certainly the exception, and association members are highly unlikely to find one readily at hand.

Tales of Unrealized Potential

The fictional scenarios that follow are drawn from hundreds of real-life examples. These all-too-common scenarios will be familiar to many readers, who—whether board members or chief executive officers—are likely to be living one or another of these dramas at the moment. Taken together, they tell a sad tale of frustrated intent and unrealized potential. And chief executives take heed! Even if the danger is not clear and present, every one of these scenarios is fraught with the peril of blame and retribution.

Alliance for the Advancement of Automation in Education

The executive committee of the Alliance for the Advancement of Automation in Education (AAAE), a national nonprofit association, is meeting at an O'Hare airport hotel for a half-day. The time of the university and college presidents and vice presidents who comprise the committee is obviously precious, and so the agenda for this quarterly meeting has been meticulously planned. The president of AAAE opens the meeting with a half-hour presentation of her vision and goals for the upcoming year, after which the executive director updates the group on his major undertakings over the past quarter, including a detailed explanation of his new organization structure. The report of the conference committee chair leads to lively discussion of ways to make sure that the next annual conference at least breaks even. Conference planning is fun, and so ideas abound—on location, marketing, cost, types of concurrent and plenary sessions, and so on for an hour.

Everyone has put in his or her two cents, everybody has found the discussion interesting and fun, no particular decisions have been made, but a general consensus has emerged. After the break, the three associate directors present their reports—a highly detailed balance sheet and income/expense analysis and comprehensive accomplishments reports from the other two executive team members. The reports are well crafted and lead to interesting discussion. AAAE executive committee members fly back home feeling well treated and fully informed. All reports were carefully prepared and capably presented, and lunch was elegant, to boot. It is hard to pin down what they have contributed to AAAE, but there is no question the committee is on top of things.

Metropolis Chamber of Commerce

The monthly meeting of the Metropolis Chamber of Commerce basically consists of progress reports from several program committees, such as port development, conventions, international trade, civic affairs, and downtown development. Today's meeting also includes adoption of the detailed line-item budget recommended by the finance committee.

Considerable discussion develops around the chamber's membership fee structure, in light of a planned deficit for the coming year; line items for staff training and out-of-state travel are especially closely scrutinized. A couple of board members point out that it's difficult to do anything important with a finished line-item budget without a framework of clear directions and priorities, but time does not permit much discussion. The budget is adopted with no substantive changes, and chamber board members go their individual ways, some with the nagging thought that they have again focused on arranging the proverbial deck chairs while the ship heads in no particular direction. They are clearly crew, not captain on the voyage.

State Training Professionals Association

The board of the State Training Professionals Association has invested a $100,000 foundation grant in a consultant firm's preparation of a strategic long-range plan for the association over the past six months. There's no question that a very thorough job has been done. Board and staff members have been interviewed, considerable information on local needs and resources has been collected and analyzed, existing association programs have been rigorously assessed, and the consultant has prepared a technically impressive document. A crisp mission statement and broad statement of goals are followed by recommended specific objectives in three program areas and an implementation schedule. Handsomely bound and printed, the association's strategic plan is well received by the board, which has set aside a Saturday morning in August for review and discussion. The consultant responds positively to several suggestions for improvement in the text and graphics and promises that the final draft will incorporate them. The board has been an appreciative audience, and the Saturday session ends on time.

National Association of Family Counselors

On the plane headed for the quarterly meeting of the board of the National Association of Family Counselors, Cheryl finds herself vaguely depressed and sorely tempted to have a couple of unneeded cocktails. She had been so excited some eighteen months ago when asked to become a board member of an organization in which she has been so active and for which she feels so much passion. Now she wonders what she has gotten herself into. Certainly the experience thus far has been disappointing. She recalls the half-day orientation session, which beautifully conveyed the association's vision and mission and explained its operating strategies, but said almost nothing about the board's role and functions. The job is to make policy, Cheryl assumes, whatever that means.

What it seems to mean is reviewing the hefty packet of paper that arrives at her office without fail a couple of weeks before every board meeting. Nothing if not conscientious, Cheryl diligently reads every word of every packet even if it means playing the masochist and taking the blob of paper to bed with her. Is asking questions about what she's read the sum of her policy-making role? Cheryl wonders. Even there, she feels stymied. The couple of times in board meetings that she has raised important questions, she has gotten the distinct impression that she has stepped over an invisible line. One of the longer-tenured trustees, managing partner of one of the country's largest law firms, has on more than one occasion observed that Cheryl may want to stick around for a while longer and "learn the ropes" before she ventures further into criticism.

Overton Women's Civic Club

The Overton Women's Civic Club has a proud 80-year tradition of serving the community, in areas such as education and neighborhood development, while providing its members with diverse social and networking opportunities. The club's Women Mentoring Women Program has been an outstanding success since its inception last year, and the civic issues forum has drawn large audiences and actually broken even for three years.

But in the context of this venerable history and current success, the club's board has grown increasingly uneasy and dissatisfied with its role. Everything seems to flow bottom-up with no clear sense of overall direction and no practical way for the board to choose among competing priorities. For 80 years, elected vice presidents—volunteers all—have headed committees that play a hands-on role in club program operations, such as the civic forum and education committees. With only two full-time staff members, a hands-on approach to board work has been essential.

The structure may have worked well at one time, when full-time volunteers—typically the wives of successful professionals and business owners—comprised the board. Now, virtually every board member holds a full-time job in addition to her board responsibilities. And with so much time spent in hands-on work, board members have little time to govern the affairs of the whole organization. True, some successful programs have been launched, but several have fizzled out over the same period from inadequate planning and oversight. Growth appears to be driven more by individual interest and initiative than by conscious board direction.

In Summary: All Roar, No Bite

The boards that appear in the foregoing scenarios are a lot of things: conscientious, hard working, capably supported by staff, provided with ample information, and probably well dressed and well behaved as well. They are also unexcited if not bored, and growing more frustrated by the day. What they are not is powerful. Declawed and defanged, these governance "beasts" appear ferocious, but their keepers know better. Displayed in a natural setting and not obviously caged, their occasional roars may fool spectators, but their governance bite is no real threat. In what major ways have these majestic creatures that roam the nonprofit association terrain been hamstrung?

Unclear Roles

Above all else, their roles and functions have never been explicitly defined. They have no vision of the governance they intend to exercise, nor specific governance objectives they intend to achieve within their vision. They "make policy," but no one is sure exactly what that is and how it is produced. What is known is that they reside at the apex of the nonprofit association pyramid and that the buck ultimately stops there. But no one is sure what to do with it when it arrives.

Reactive Approach

These hard-working boards are basically reactive in their approach to governance. Rather than taking the initiative in generating unique bottom-line results for their organizations, these boards tend to react to finished staff work, to follow rather than lead. The Metropolis Chamber's finished budget and the State Training Professionals Association's consultant-produced strategic plan are classic pathological examples. This "thumbing through" approach to governance cannot possibly take full advantage of the experience, wisdom, talent, expertise, and creativity that board members bring to the governance job. Nor can it build enthusiasm, commitment, and ownership among board members, who are more bystanders than participants in serious decision making.

Focused on Minor Details

In lieu of a well-defined governance role that provides high-level work, our diligent boards, intending to contribute something concrete, inevitably involve themselves in relatively minor operational details at the expense of more critical issues, and in deliberations that bore their members and erode enthusiasm and commitment. Witness the AAAE board's detailed attention to annual conference preparation. As John Carver observes in his *Boards that Make a Difference*, such boards "expend their energy on a host of demonstrably less important, even trivial items."

Instead of impassioned discussion about the changes to be produced in their world, board members are ordinarily found passively listening to staff reports or dealing with personnel procedures and the budget line for out-of-state travel.

Not Structured to Govern

The Metropolis Chamber of Commerce and Overton Women's City Club scenarios illustrate a common structural flaw: being driven by programmatic and operational committees that make it well nigh impossible to exercise associationwide, top-down influence. The Metropolis Chamber's port development, conventions, and international trade committees and the Overton Women's City Club's civic forum and education committees are all narrow program committees that neither rise above nor cut across the whole organization.

Such committee structures, common in volunteer-driven associations, lead to board members being so busy operating, *owning*, and lobbying for specific programs that they cannot possibly put the overall association's interests first. Indeed, the proverbial trees loom much larger than the forest, which is often seen dimly, if at all.

From Frustration to Retribution

From my interviews with thousands of nonprofit board members over the past fifteen years, I am convinced that these tales of unrealized potential are very much the rule, not the exception. If the reader is puzzled and frustrated in his or her work on an association board, join the crowd. Sprinkled throughout pages of interview notes are words and phrases such as "pointless," "confusing," "a waste of my time," "hard to stay awake," and the plaintive "there must be more than this." Indeed, it is nothing short of a miracle—and testimony to the deep-seated desire to contribute—that so many nonprofit association board members have so patiently endured for so long.

Very often frustration builds up to the point where it cannot be contained. Unfortunately, the result is often the swift punishment of the hapless chief executive of the moment, who is summarily sent packing. Such retribution, while it may provide a satisfying catharsis, is not likely to lead to strengthened governance. Missing the point, it merely starts another cycle of futility on its way.

Why So Many Ineffective Boards?

What accounts for the widespread ineffectiveness of nonprofit association boards? Peter Drucker points out that nonprofits have tended to borrow from the for-profit sector and that "little that is so far available to the non-profit institutions to help them with their leadership and management has been specifically designed for them." It is also obvious that far more attention has been paid to executive management in both the business and nonprofit sectors than to governance, which has tended to be an afterthought. As Carver observes, nonprofit governing boards have been "understudied and underdeveloped," leading to a "flagrant irony in management literature: *Where opportunity for leadership is greatest, job design for leadership is poorest.*"

Adversarial Model

The prevailing nonprofit governance models have also been inadequate to the task, and perhaps the adversarial model is the preeminent culprit. The history of public boards and legislative bodies in America has exercised a deleterious influence on the development of nonprofit governance. Motivated by a checks and balances philosophy, public boards and legislative bodies have generally taken an adversarial approach to their governance tasks. The "critters" are to be closely watched, and if the "critters" are left to their own devices, who knows what abuses of power will occur.

Chief executives cutting their teeth in this adversarial environment have naturally learned to take a defensive, control-oriented position vis a vis their boards. Creativity and candor are not virtues in such an environment; learning to keep the board from meddling in executive and administrative affairs *is.* Therefore, generations of executives have been taught that the only safe approach is to keep their boards so busy reacting to finished staff work that they will not have time to dig into affairs that are not their business.

Board-As-Passive-Audience Model

Another common model that does not work is what I think of as the board-as-audience. In this model, the nonprofit board basically receives a flow of paper from below, which it reviews and occasionally acts on. Spending considerable time thumbing through finished documents, the audience-board exerts little front-end, proactive influence on organizational affairs, feels little ownership for the decisions it does make, and tends to bore its members to death over time.

Volunteer Career Ladder Model

A third common but unproductive model is the board as the top rung of the career development ladder. Seen frequently in the association field, the career development board is based on the assumption that experience as a volunteer in an association, and moving through the various volunteering experiences, is the appropriate preparation for service on the board of directors. The fact is, while commitment to, empathy for, and knowledge of association operations are useful attributes, volunteering in association affairs outside the board does not prepare a volunteer to be a strong board member. Skill in managing a volunteer activity may have little if any to do with the requirements of governance. Another inadequacy of this model is the tendency for boards to become inbred because they lack the broader perspective that "outsiders" can bring to the board's work.

Lowered Expectations

In the absence of an effective board governance model and in the face of chief executive resistance, it can be extraordinarily difficult for a board to strengthen its governance role. In practice, new members join boards one-by-one, often with only the most rudimentary knowledge of governance roles and responsibilities. No matter how frustrating they may find their board experience, newcomers are highly unlikely to be vocal critics of established routines.

Some, disillusioned and discouraged, eventually fade away. Unfortunately, many who remain merely lower their governance expectations, assuming that low-level pain and suffering are the price of volunteering. And too many of these survivors settle for learning the ropes and expanding their personal influence without strengthening governance. Indeed, these "good old boys and gals" who have gained influence through longevity can be a major barrier to building a more effective nonprofit board since they more often than not see board reform as personally threatening.

Board Empowerment

   Fortunately, association board members and chief executives need not be bound by tradition and the shackles of past practice in their governance work. They need not be a victim of frustration that builds to surrender or destructive anger. If they are willing to work closely together, and to expend the required time and energy, they can move beyond inheritance to *board empowerment*. They can create a board that truly leads, rather than merely reacting and responding to staff. They can create a board that not only generates powerful results for the organization it governs, but also provides its members with the satisfaction and self-fulfillment that they want and to which they are entitled in return for their contribution of time and energy. The path to governance empowerment is *board design*, a powerful process that is introduced in the next chapter.

Chapter Three
Designing Your Own Board

Beyond Inheritance

Inheriting an association board created by our forebears and passing it on relatively unchanged to our successors is a strategy that, at best, is likely to miss an opportunity to participate in *creating* a board whose role, structure, and process are tailored both to the association's needs and to the needs and expectations of the board members themselves. At its worst, inheritance is a recipe for unrealized board members' potential, disappointment and anger, and often cathartic release—usually aimed at the chief executive of the moment. Inheritance cannot take into account changing association circumstances and needs or the changing cast on the board, or take advantage of the diverse resources—in the form of experience, expertise, and networks—that board members bring to the governance task.

Self-Determination

Design is a kind of governance *self-determination* that is aimed at ensuring that:

- A governing board is capable of making the most powerful contribution feasible to achieving the vision and mission of the association it is responsible for governing.
- The board's processes meet the needs and expectations of individual board members, thereby building enthusiasm and commitment.

The board leadership design process enables association board members, in creative alliance with their chief executive and his or her executive team members, to determine precisely what kind of board will meet the needs of their association and satisfy the expectations of the board members themselves: what the board will achieve, how the board will go about producing its "products" and carrying out its governance responsibilities, and also what the process of serving on the board will be like.

Without engaging in a conscious, systematic design process, a board is likely to be captive to outmoded notions of "good" and "bad" governance and to preconceptions that have gone untested through the years. A board not actively participating in its own design is also less likely to be open to, or to capitalize on, recent advances in the field of nonprofit leadership.

Ownership and Team Building

In addition to its obvious substantive benefits, a conscious board design process that actively engages board members and their chief executive officer is also a powerful way of building board members' *ownership* of the governance process, thereby strengthening their commitment to the board and its responsibilities. Another side benefit of design is the team building that inevitably occurs when board members engage in an intensive process with powerful outcomes. Working together to create significant results, rather than merely ratifying others' thinking, builds teams in two ways. It tells participants a lot about each other—how they think, their interpersonal skills, their knowledge and perspectives—and it builds experience in working together on important matters. This experience can help in building a model for addressing thorny issues in the future.

A Practical Process

Designing your own board, or, if you will, fashioning a *board leadership design*, may at first blush appear somewhat theoretical and even a little pie-in-the-sky. After all, the proverbial train is running, isn't it? How can we halt it at high speed without disruption or even derailment? To be sure, some concentrated time will be required to develop a *board leadership design*, preferably at least a full day in a retreat setting away from the hurly-burly. But this need not be disruptive, since any board, anywhere, can find a day if it looks far enough ahead.

More importantly, the board leadership design need not involve radical, one-fell-swoop change at a pace that exhausts and discombobulates participants. The *consenting adult* principle is at work here: No board need change anything it does not want to change, or move any faster than it wants to move. Nothing prevents a board from retaining the valuable practices of the past—those that have worked well and that clearly meet present and future governance needs—while adding enhancements intended to strengthen the board's leadership.

Another facet of the design process that will keep a board firmly grounded in reality is the ability to draw not only on its own history of effective practice, but also on the rapidly growing literature reporting what other boards have learned. Intelligent borrowing, based on a clear understanding of needs, expectations, and circumstances, always makes sense in the design process, and these days there is much more accumulated wisdom to draw on than even a decade ago.

The Chief Executive's Role

Although part-time volunteers serving on an association board may feel frustrated and disappointed about their governance role, they may not recognize, much less act on, the need to redesign their board. Rather than letting the need go unmet, and falling victim to the inevitable spontaneous combustion caused by unalleviated frustration, a savvy chief executive will take a leading role in initiating the design process.

Practical steps that a chief executive can take to ensure that his or her board undertakes its own design include:

- making board members aware of both the design need and the choice, principally by sharing pertinent written material
- working closely with the board chair to build a "critical mass" of board support for engaging in the design process
- playing a strong supportive role, helping to structure and stage the design effort, to facilitate the process, and to prepare the required documentation
- helping to ensure that the resulting board leadership design is actually implemented.

The bottom line is that chief executives cannot afford to take "no" for an answer where design is concerned. The fact is that they are quite likely to be held accountable for their boards' lackluster performance and growing frustration, even if the real culprit is failure to fashion a leadership design.

Design Principles

For the process of developing a board leadership design that meets the needs of a particular association to produce the intended results, it must be guided by six key principles (Figure 1):

1. **Accountability**—Board members must explicitly take accountability for the performance of their board, looking to themselves to define what the board aspires to be and how it wants to operate.

2. **Bottom-Line Focus**—A board should be seen as a kind of business within the wider nonprofit association that has unique bottom lines that must drive the design of its structure and process. Otherwise, a board is likely to embrace solutions (say, a particular committee structure or an approach to strategic planning) that do not fit the board. Without the bottom lines to guide the design process, it is all too easy to fall prey to pet notions of *right* and *wrong* governance.

3. **Openness**—Board members participating in the design process must be free of preconceptions about *good* and *bad* boards and must wipe the slate clean of the conventional wisdom that has been inherited from the past.

4. **Uniqueness**—The design process is most productive when it is tailored to the unique circumstances, capabilities, and needs of particular association boards, and when it is recognized that other associations' board designs cannot be borrowed carte blanche. This does not mean, of course, that an association's design will not benefit from the lessons of successful experience.

5. **Dynamism**—Boards that are serious about their own leadership design know that there is no design for all time; as association circumstances, capabilities, and needs evolve, so should the board leadership design. It makes the best of sense to periodically examine the design and determine how it needs to be changed to ensure that it matches reality.

6. **Collaboration**—Even though a board must take explicit accountability for determining what it will be and do, the design process works best when the chief executive officer and his or her top executives are involved intensively with the board in developing the design. Not only will their knowledge be a valuable contribution to the process, their understanding and ownership will be critical to implementing the design. *In reality, as part-time volunteers, association board members depend on staff to provide much of the time and energy required for implementation of the design.*

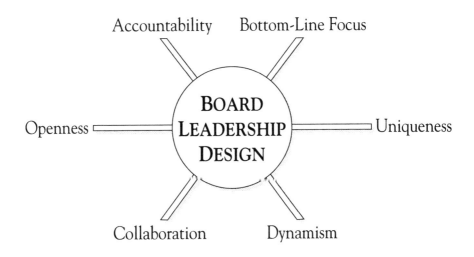

Figure 1. Design Principles

Design Cannot Be Delegated

Boards that are serious about the design of their governance role will take the time to do the job themselves, with the participation and collaboration of the chief executive and his or her top staff. Neither asking staff to prepare and present the design, nor hiring a consultant to study the board and present design recommendations is likely to produce satisfactory results.

An effective approach is to set aside at least a full day for the design purpose, preferably in a retreat setting with a professional facilitator without a vested interest in particular design outcomes. This approach will ensure not only that the resulting board leadership design truly reflects board members' thinking, but also that board members feel the degree of ownership and commitment that will fuel implementation of the design in subsequent weeks and months.

Design Elements

In a nutshell, the board design process involves developing in detail three major points on the "design triangle" (see Figure 2):

1. **The Board's Leadership Mission**—The leadership mission consists of detailed statements that describe the outcomes that the board intends to produce, both for the association and for the board members themselves; the roles that the board must play to produce these outcomes; and the board's culture, in terms of the values that should govern board members' interactions and the individual return that board members can reasonably expect on their investment of time and energy in their board service.

2. **The Board's Structure and Process**—Structure and process are concerned with the organization of the board's work. Questions to be addressed here are the committee structure, the meeting schedule, the method of developing board agendas, and the specifics of the board's participation in such mainline association processes as strategic planning, preparation of the annual operational plan and budget, performance monitoring, and financial resource development.

3. **Required Resources**—Of course, it means little to articulate lofty goals and to launch ambitious processes without the careful estimation of the resources required to carry out the processes and the explicit commitment of these resources. The preeminent resource is without doubt the board members themselves, and the design must consider both the composition of the board and the board members' time that is required. Staff support for the board is another key resource. Extraordinary resource requirements might include retaining a consultant to facilitate a strategic planning retreat or funding a membership

Figure 2. Board Leadership Design

satisfaction survey as part of the planning process. Explicitly committing resources as part of the design process ensures that the association board and staff do not engage in wishful thinking, important initiatives do not collapse midstream, and dashed expectations do not dampen enthusiasm and commitment.

Identifying Design Gaps

The board's leadership mission is truly the driver of the design process. Based on the detailed leadership mission, a board that is seriously engaged in designing itself will inevitably identify some gaps in achieving its mission, which will enable it to devise enhancements in structure and process to fill the gaps. To attempt to upgrade its leadership structure and process without the context of a detailed leadership mission and without having identified gaps, a board can easily fall prey to unquestioned conventional wisdom and to individual board members' pet solutions and preconceived notions. Solutions that address no specific issues or problems are notorious for wasting time and other precious resources while disappointing participants and eroding their commitment.

Let us say, for example, that a board decides that one of the key elements of its leadership mission is to determine its association's vision for the future. If no vision has been, or is being, developed, or the board has not actively participated in shaping the vision that does exist, then a *design gap* clearly exists. Filling such gaps is basically what designing board structure and process is all about. To address this particular gap, the board will want to work closely with the chief executive officer and executive team in fashioning a process that involves the board in a meaningful fashion in shaping an association vision that consists of specific elements and attributes. This will almost certainly entail the design of a full-fledged strategic planning (or strategic management) process that includes vision clarification as a key step. (See Chapter 9 for a detailed description of the planning process.)

Implementing the Design

The finished board leadership mission, and the accompanying structural and procedural enhancements aimed at more fully accomplishing the mission, should be committed to writing in a formal design document and eventually formally adopted by the full board as a major policy statement. This policy statement should convey the elements of the board leadership mission in detail and clearly describe each of the enhancements in structure and process that are intended to translate the mission into practice.

Implementation of major structural and procedural enhancements is likely to be a highly complex process that requires detailed implementation planning and coordination if it is not to fall apart midstream. For example, launching a new standing committee structure may require amending an association's bylaws, and will certainly entail such steps as fashioning detailed committee charges, identifying committee chairs and members, orienting the committees on their roles and responsibilities. Practical ways to manage this demanding change process are discussed in Chapter 13.

Keeping the Design Up-to-Date

Effective board leadership designs are dynamic, changing periodically to reflect changing circumstances, innovations in the governance field, and new participants in the governance process. One useful technique for keeping the board leadership design up-to-date is an annual one or one-and-a-half-day board-executive staff retreat, perhaps combining association strategic planning activities with the governance design job (See Chapter 12 for a detailed discussion of retreat design). Another useful approach is to assign to one of the board's standing committees oversight of the design process as a major responsibility. The use of the board's executive committee for this purpose is discussed in Chapter 7. Such a committee would ensure that the annual re-design retreat is well planned and executed.

Design and the Board-Staff Partnership

Engaging in a detailed board leadership design process involving the chief executive officer and executive team members as well as the board provides a significant opportunity for the *creative division of labor* between board and staff. The challenge is to go beyond relatively meaningless guidelines (the policy-administration distinction, for example) and to rise above defensiveness in shaping roles in the best interest of the association.

How deeply the board will become involved in the "innards" of an association function such as planning will be negotiated by the board and staff as part of the governance design process. Guiding the negotiation will be various factors, including association circumstances, the board's leadership mission, and staff capability, among others. An association with a large staff and well-developed planning process will be able to involve its board at a higher level in making planning decisions than an association that has limited staff and is less well developed. In the latter instance, the need for board expertise in fashioning plans may be critical and justify more detailed involvement.

The point is, there is no definition of the appropriate balance of power between board and staff that will serve for all time. The balance should be viewed as dynamic, requiring regular, high-level renegotiation as an integral part of the design process.

Common Resistance to Designing Boards

Association board members and executives interested in becoming involved in the development of a board leadership design should anticipate resistance of various kinds. The following situations are commonly encountered (see Figure 3).

DESIGN RESISTANCE

Inertia	Absence of Vision	Time Worries	Vested Interest

Board Leadership Design

Figure 3. Design Resistance

Inertia

The familiar is always attractive, and the specter of change can be threatening. Even if current practices are less than perfect, and perhaps even involve some pain, they are known. We have learned to live with them, we know their good and bad features, and we can't really be sure what change will bring, no matter how well planned; after all, things could get worse. Inertia also relates to a conservative "If it ain't broke, don't fix it" or "Let well enough alone" attitude. Although sounding sensibly skeptical and down to earth (as in, "I'm not about to be hoodwinked by some huckster peddling the latest fad"), all too often what is behind this resistance is a reluctance to experience the discomfort of growth and development.

Absence of Vision

Board members typically have come to their governance roles with little formal preparation, and their day-to-day lives often involve little attention to the field of nonprofit governance beyond their actual work on the board. So unless they have gone through some kind of board training and development process, they may be unaware of the opportunities to heighten board impact. They just plain don't know that there is more to life in the governance realm.

Time Worries

Board members are usually ambitious, successful people who lead full and busy lives outside of their board work. The first thought that will occur to many of these fully engaged people when strengthening board governance is raised as a possibility is that more of their time will be demanded. The thought of becoming even busier can cause serious resistance to change, no matter how committed the board member is to the association.

Vested Interest

Perhaps the most insidious and deeply ingrained resistance to change is driven by the vested interest of one or more board members in the board's current structure and operations. The fact is, board members whose commitment to either their association's welfare or to their own advancement, or both, is strong enough, who are tenacious, and whose threshold of frustration and pain is high enough will be able to advance to positions of influence on a board, no matter what its structural and procedural deficiencies. They have, frankly, worked tremendously hard to make the board work. They have *learned the ropes* and in the process become a kind of inner circle, or *old guard*. Since such board members are typically truly committed to the association and are sincerely conscientious in carrying out their board responsibilities, they can easily fail to recognize the selfish nature of their opposition. They are conscious only that changes threaten a world to which they are deeply attached.

Launching a Design Process

Essential to getting the board leadership design process underway is a cadre of *change champions* who are willing to face the inevitable resistance in order to secure the commitment of a majority on the board to move forward. Ideally, the hard core of this cadre will consist of the board chair, the chief executive officer, and one or more of the *old guard* members who can overcome their resistance.

The goal of these change champions is to convince a majority of their colleagues on the board that it will make sense to spend intensive time addressing ways to strengthen the board's leadership. Merely asking, "Would you like to have a retreat for this purpose?" will more often than not receive a "no" answer with little hesitation. And God forbid that being trained to be a more effective board should even be hinted at!

A well-thought-out strategy to sell the idea is almost always required. Approaches that tend to work in this regard are:

- supplying board members with pertinent readings that make the case for board development and chronicle real-life developmental experiences, and, if possible, exposing board members to presentations that will whet their appetites, say at conferences or workshops

- emphasizing the self-determination aspect of board governance design and the "let's get more out of the experience if we're spending the time, anyway" attitude

- assuring everyone that, in keeping with the "consenting adults" philosophy, nothing really bad can happen over the objection of the board

- making clear that this will not be another one of those "teachy-preachy" board training programs that merely goes over the little golden rules for well-behaved boards

When it appears that a majority of the board is willing to engage in a leadership design process, then a formal resolution stating the intent and specifically committing to a retreat for this purpose should be adopted. Ideally, the vote will be unanimous, but to wait for unanimity can be unrealistic, and to allow the opposition of a few to scuttle the design process would be foolish. Experience has taught that there is often a small core that cannot be convinced to engage in a change process, no matter how compelling the arguments for doing so. The good news is that, once involved, they are likely to see the utility and to participate, if somewhat grudgingly.

Of course, getting a board together with its chief executive and executive team for a day or so to deal with such an unfamiliar subject as board leadership design is by its very nature a complex, high-stakes affair involving significant risk for the "change champions" who pushed for the event. If not meticulously planned and led, such a retreat could fall apart, causing more harm than if it had never been held in the first place. Practical ways to ensure that design retreats work—that they achieve their aims fully at an acceptable cost—are discussed in Chapter 12.

Chapter Four
The Board Leadership Mission

Driver of Board Design

Keep in mind that an association board is far more than merely the pinnacle of the association pyramid. In a very real sense the board is an *organizational entity* within its association—a kind of *enterprise* within the parent corporation. As an enterprise within its corporate family, it should be guided by a clear, detailed mission that tells what it is all about, in terms of its intended impacts, the roles it will play in producing these impacts, and its internal culture (see Figure 4).

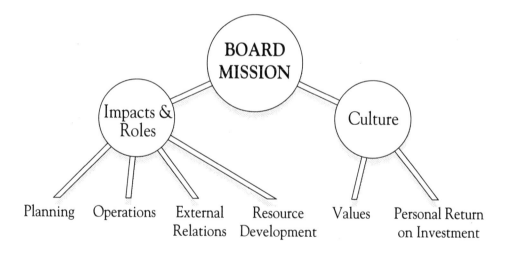

Figure 4. Board Leadership Mission

Some readers may at this point be tempted to say, "Stop right here. You're making a mountain out of a molehill. It's clear what a board is supposed to do; its job is to be a board. A board's a board, dammit!"

Well, on reflection, we know this is far too simplistic. There are all kinds of boards, from proactive and creatively involved in leading to passive and uncreatively involved in following. Only by starting with a clear board leadership mission can a board find its place in the galaxy of boards, creating its own unique identity and distinguishing itself from all other association boards.

A board's leadership mission is the preeminent driver of its own design process. Without a clear leadership mission, a board has no basis for the determination of its governance structure and the processes that it will employ in carrying out its governance responsibilities. Without knowing what it intends to produce for the association, what impacts it wants to have, an association board cannot sensibly decide what committees it should have, how often it should meet, the specific roles it should play in strategic planning and budget preparation, to name some of the more important decisions that will determine what kind of board it will be. More than any other factor, a board's leadership mission frees it from merely carrying past practices and pet approaches uncritically into the future. *Mission makes board self-determination possible*.

Skip No Steps

Board members and association executives tend to be very busy people with a keen desire to get going rather than talking, and so there will be a temptation to skip over the mission formulation phase of the board leadership design process. However, jumping too soon into the nuts and bolts questions, such as board size and number of committees—without a clear framework—will risk half-baked solutions to vague problems.

Many, if not most, association boards are doing many things right, and we have numerous examples of best practices and published prescriptions on which to draw. Despite this, it is essential that a board that is committed to strengthening its governance take the time to go through the mission formulation phase of the design process completely, skipping no steps. We have all learned from experience that the phrase, "It goes without saying," is often applied to something that is unclear, little understood, and badly needing to be said. Only by identifying gaps in producing the outcomes we want can we reliably fashion the structural and procedural enhancements to fill the gaps. Otherwise, we are all too likely to fall prey to pet structural and procedural solutions that are unconnected to serious governance gaps that need to be filled.

Internal and External Influences

An association board and its chief executive will exert considerable influence in fashioning the board's leadership vision. However, a number of external factors must be taken into account. There are always the legal requirements that a nonprofit corporate board must satisfy, along with pertinent legislation and regulations. Far more important, of course, are the vision, strategic directions, and needs of the association itself. For example, if an association is going through an aggressive growth and diversification phase, it may very well need a board that focuses more attention on external relations, stakeholder management, and resource development than on performance oversight.

Use a Retreat Setting

Crafting a board leadership mission is hardly the stuff of day-to-day operations. Radically different from the normal business, and demanding intensive attention, the mission is best fashioned in a retreat setting, as part of the board design process. In the process of formulating a board leadership mission in a retreat setting, a free-flowing, brain-storming process makes good sense. By fashioning lists—say, of possible board outcomes in the area of planning, operations, and external relations—as a starting point, participants in the design process can ensure that all ideas and viewpoints are taken into consideration. At this stage of the process, undue discipline—looking for right answers and choosing among possibilities—is a vice that will inhibit participation, quell enthusiasm, and limit the exploration of possibilities.

If the initial board design retreat is seen as a "jump start" mechanism intended to generate opportunities for stronger board leadership, then a follow-up process involving analysis, choice, and commitment can be built in. At the very least, the job of cleaning up and analyzing the content of the retreat might be assigned to an ad hoc board committee, which might also be accountable for fashioning detailed change recommendations for full board consideration and action. This role might also be assigned to the consultant who facilitated the design retreat.

Process Spin-Offs

Engaging in an intensive board mission formulation process will produce significant process spinoffs in addition to the mission itself. Over and over again, boards that have taken the time to go through such a demanding process, away from the boardroom, have become a more cohesive and effective governance team. They have gotten to know and understand each other better and have learned new ways to work together.

Another side benefit is the strength of the commitment that comes from producing, and thereby owning, their own governance mission. It is one thing to be taught something, or to have it brought to us in a well-crafted document; at best, we will be intellectually committed to what we have learned. It is another to devote time, sweat, and sometimes tears to a production, to which we will have a deeper attachment based on our truly owning it.

Outcomes and Roles

In developing the outcomes and roles elements of its leadership mission, an association board will engage in a two-step process:

- first identifying the major impacts it intends to have in major governance areas
- then identifying major roles that it might play in achieving these impacts

Board impacts and roles can be organized by major governance areas: planning, operations, external relations, financial resource development, and leadership and management of the board itself. Keep in mind that these impacts are in virtually every instance a joint production of the board, its chief executive officer, and executive team members. The point is not that the impacts are the exclusive production of the board alone; rather, it is that the board plays a major creative role in producing them, rather than merely thumbing through finished plans for achieving the outcomes that are fed to it by staff.

Outcomes and Roles in the Planning Realm

The realm of planning offers perhaps the greatest opportunity for a board to impact the affairs of its association (see Chapter 9). The governance impacts that boards I have worked with have identified in this area include: an association with a clear vision for the future and detailed strategic directions; an association that is responsive to changing member needs; an association whose strategies, structures, and programs are in sync with environmental change; an association that is growing in membership and revenues; diversification of an association's programs, products, and services; the systematic allocation of resources to higher priority programs; the systematic elimination of programs that are less productive or have lower growth potential; an association that is fiscally sound; an association that is guided by clear and detailed annual objectives; and an association with a balanced budget.

The reader should keep in mind that we are discussing desired practical impacts or outcomes of the work of an association board itself on its association, not the impact of that association on its wider world. Our association board must answer the question—What will result from our efforts?—if it is to play a creative role in guiding those efforts. Only by exploring its own possible impacts and deciding its own priorities can an association board design its own structure and processes.

Having defined the impacts that it anticipates playing a major part in producing in the planning realm—in creative partnership with the chief executive officer and staff—an association board can then consider the major roles that it might play in the production of these outcomes. For example:

- in *strategic* planning, an association board might identify as key roles fashioning a clear set of association values, a vision statement, and a mission; setting priorities and growth targets; and adopting strategies to achieve the targets.
- in *operational* planning, an association board might see as key roles the negotiation of annual performance objectives with major operating unit/program heads, the approval of revenue and expenditure targets for the upcoming fiscal year, and the adoption of a balanced budget.

Operational Matters

Some traditional association chief executives will shudder with horror over the specter of board dabbling in administrative matters. However, even the most resistant chief executive will, on second thought, see powerful impacts in this area that demand creative, in-depth board participation. For example, three possible impacts are:

- strong chief executive leadership
- the achievement of strategic and operational goals
- operation within budget

In achieving such important impacts, an association board's roles might include selection of the chief executive officer, evaluation of chief executive performance against established performance targets, and monitoring fiscal and program performance against plan.

External Relations

An association board's impacts in external relations might include: a clear association image, wider public understanding of and support for the association, and stronger relationships with key stakeholder organizations (defined as organizations with actual or potential influence on the association's mission, strategies, and operations). Producing such impacts might involve a board in fashioning its association's preferred image, overseeing development of public relations and marketing strategies, and playing a hands-on role in speaking on behalf of the association and in building positive relationships with selected stakeholder organizations.

Financial Resource Development

Possible impacts in this area are: diversification and growth of sources of revenue; closer relationships with revenue sources, especially grant makers; and money itself. In achieving these outcomes, an association board might require financial contributions of itself, fund and oversee a formal financial resource development function, adopt annual resource development priorities and targets, and personally approach funders on behalf of the association.

Board Culture

An association board's culture plays a major role in determining what it is like to be a member of that particular board. Is the experience interesting, exciting, fun? Or is serving on the board a deflating experience, all payment and little return? Over time, a board that does not explicitly define the culture that it wants to build—and fashion the structure and process to build it—will find recruiting and retaining capable members much more difficult.

The two key components of a board's culture are:

- the *values* that guide its work as a board and the interactions of its members
- the board members' *return on investment* (ROI)—the specific returns that board members as individuals can legitimately expect from their investment of time and energy in board affairs

Board Values

Despite the conventional wisdom, values are anything but self-evident. And unless they are made explicit, they cannot be incorporated into the design of board structure and process. If they are left implicit, puzzling dysfunctions in board deliberations may occur that have no obvious basis.

Values that boards have developed to guide their work include: commitment to the vision and mission of the association; putting the interests of the association above personal interests in making decisions; publicly identifying conflicts of interest and removing oneself from the decision process in such instances; dealing with each other in a respectful, civil fashion; being open and candid and avoiding hidden agendas; promoting full participation and avoiding cliques; having a diverse board, in race and gender.

Individual ROI

The concept of a personal ROI will appear strange and perhaps self-serving to many association board members. But, as Cyril Houle has so rightly pointed out, "Proper attention to motivation is . . . essential after people have joined a board." Motivation is not merely a matter of calling board members' attention to the higher ends to which their work contributes; it also has to do with meeting legitimate needs that are less altruistic and often closely bound up with members' egos. There is absolutely no reason why such needs should conflict with broader association needs. Indeed, by making needs visible and explicit, an association board can ensure that they are integrated with the board's other higher purposes in the design of structure and process.

Examples of legitimate expectations for personal return include: board meetings that are interesting and occasionally even fun; administrative support that facilitates understanding of important issues; opportunities for networking; opportunities to grow socially and professionally; pride in making a major impact; full use of one's experience, skills, and capabilities on the board; public exposure and attention.

Applying Cultural Standards

Culture often appears to be a vague and even "flaky" matter with limited potential for practical impact. However, it can be a powerful lever for developing association board leadership if it is taken seriously. A practical approach to ensuring its utility is to ask and answer in detail in the annual design session how values and individual expectations are being addressed by current structure and process. Major gaps, and hence sources of dysfunction, can thereby be identified and corrective action taken in the design process.

Summary and Coming Attractions

Chapters 3 and 4 have taken a brief look at the key elements in developing a *board leadership design*, including fashioning a clear, detailed *leadership mission*; identifying *structure* and *process* enhancements aimed at promoting fuller achievement of the mission; and committing the required *resources* to carry out the required structure and process. Without a detailed leadership design, the structure and process that an association board uses to do its governance work is far more likely to reflect preconceived notions of what a *good* board is and pet solutions to undefined issues.

One of the most important outcomes of the design process is the creative division of labor between board and staff, going beyond theoretical black-and-white distinctions and reflecting an association's real-life situation.

Section II examines the preeminent resource for successful governance—the members of the board themselves, ways to enhance the effectiveness of board members, the critical board-executive partnership, use of board committees, and other structural matters.

Section II

Organizing the Board

Chapter Five
Solving the Human Equation

People Are Paramount

Boards are first and foremost people, and more than any other factor, the people who serve on association boards determine their effectiveness. The right people can with commitment and tenacity overcome organizational deficiencies. However, no structure or system, no matter how well designed, and no chief executive, no matter how capable and hard working, can remedy serious deficiencies in board membership.

Boards members are a rich human resource to their associations, bringing to association leadership their:

- time and commitment to the association's vision and mission
- experience, knowledge, talent, and expertise
- varied perspectives on association issues
- ties to the wider world in which the association functions
- stature and political influence
- financial resources

Realizing the Promise

Assembling resources is only half the battle, and the world of nonprofit associations is replete with examples of boards that function well below capacity, cheating their associations of sorely needed leadership and their board members of the opportunity to make a powerful contribution. Capitalizing on the board as a rich human resource, translating its tremendous promise into reality, requires that the board itself take responsibility and accountability for the four key components of board human resource development:

- determining such structural matters as the length of terms, the number and allocation of seats, and the process for nomination and selection
- ensuring that the "right" people fill board seats
- managing the performance of board members
- developing the leadership capability of board members

Accountability is the key concept here. A board that does not take explicit collective accountability for developing its leadership capability and for strengthening itself as a human resource will not fulfill its promise. Fortunately, if a board does accept the challenge, taking accountability for developing itself, it can in tackling the job draw on a rapidly growing body of knowledge based on successful nonprofit experience.

Common Syndromes

Association board members and executives committed to developing the board as a human resource should be aware of common syndromes that both signal inadequate attention to board capability building and represent serious deficiencies to be remedied. Every one of the following types is harmful only when it is predominant and defines the character of a board; in small doses, they can cause little harm and may even bring benefits.

Birds-of-a-Feather Boards

Many association boards have over the years basically reproduced themselves, becoming extremely inbred at the expense of diversity in viewpoints and experience. These "birds of a feather flocking together" are typically the result of an informal selection process that relies on personal networks to supply candidates for board seats, without the guidance of a detailed description of desired board member characteristics and attributes.

Good Old Girl and Boy Boards

Boards with a small, highly influential core of members who have basically earned positions of influence through their longevity, tenacity, and high tolerance for pain are unlikely to make full use of the board as a human resource. These good old girl and boy boards are typically the result of vaguely defined roles, structure, and process. New board members, coming on the board in twos, threes, and fours, will at best become major contributors to the governance job only slowly, as they learn the ropes and earn their proverbial spurs. At worst, these newcomers, no matter what their talent and experience, are apt to become discouraged or even cynical and to fade away relatively soon. Good old girls and boys on boards naturally tend to be satisfied with things as they are; after all, they have put tremendous effort into learning how to work the governance process, whatever its flaws. They are often, therefore, stalwart enemies of change.

The Career-Ladder Board

Often seen in the world of trade associations, the career ladder board basically sees board service as the capstone of a career in the association. Board membership is an honor bestowed on association members who have successfully volunteered in various capacities in the association. An obvious benefit of the career ladder board is the in-depth knowledge of association affairs that experienced volunteers bring to the board. The problem is that volunteering to *govern* by serving on an association's board is different in kind from any other kind of volunteering. Extensive volunteer experience does not basically prepare someone to govern effectively. Indeed, experienced volunteers who have moved through the ranks are very likely to have accumulated a series of narrow experiences that do not add up to an associationwide perspective. They are highly unlikely to have acquired significant governance skills in the course of their volunteer careers.

The Representative Board

Common when association boards are elected by the membership, the representative board tends to respond to constituencies and to operate in a legislative fashion, focusing on building consensus for the primary purpose of reconciling constituency interests. Cumbersome at best, and typically narrow in focus, such boards tend not to provide strong overall corporate leadership as they build consensus from diverse constituency interests.

All of the foregoing examples represent tendencies that are pathological only when carried to an extreme and can produce important benefits when found in moderation. For example, some recognition of volunteer experience and some focus on reconciling constituency interests can strengthen an association board if kept within bounds. *The key to balance is the board's conscious, systematic management of itself as a human resource in the interest of the whole association's governance.* We now turn to the key elements of this board self-management process.

Assign Accountability

If, indeed, an association board has made a firm commitment to take accountability for managing itself as a precious resource, then it makes sense to assign specific board management accountability to a standing committee, as a means to ensure sustained, detailed attention to board management. The board's executive committee would be a likely candidate (see Chapter 7) for this role, which involves:

- ensuring that board size and composition are synchronized with an association's governance needs and its circumstances
- developing a profile of desired characteristics and attributes of board members

- identifying a more specific list of requirements when board vacancies need to be filled
- identifying likely candidates to fill board seats and assessing their suitability
- recommending the appointment of new board members
- ensuring that a comprehensive board capability building strategy is developed and overseeing its implementation
- developing detailed performance standards for board members, recommending their adoption by the full board, monitoring board members' performance against these standards, and recommending corrective action as appropriate

Board Size

Most readers are members of—or working with—established boards, and their associations' bylaws spell out the number and types of board seats, board members' terms, and the selection process. This chapter is basically concerned with practical ways to strengthen the management of these boards within the current structure without major reform: to make the selection process more effective, the capability-building strategy more productive, and the performance-management process more rigorous. However, no bylaws are intended to last forever. An association board's basic structure should be reexamined every few years to ensure that it meets the current and anticipated needs of the association.

Determining the appropriate size of a board is more art than science, and viewpoints on the *best* size widely vary. Many readers have undoubtedly heard that the only "good" board is a small one, usually meaning no more than 10 or 12 members. The guiding principles of the small-board advocates appear to be to be efficiency and convenience. Large boards will be unwieldy and cumbersome, and hence "bad," while smaller ones can accomplish their governance tasks with dispatch. So goes the efficiency logic. In fact, however, there are many examples of strong, highly effective governing boards with more than 15, 20, or even 30 members. We can easily find many examples of boards with fewer than 15 members that do not produce powerful governance results.

Basically, size alone is not a primary, or even major, determinant of board effectiveness. All we can say in the abstract is that for larger boards, diversity will be easier to achieve, and it will be more difficult to manage the logistics involved in convening and supporting the board. Conversely, the smaller a board is, the more difficult diversity will be to achieve and the easier it will be to schedule meetings and to manage and support the governance process.

Creative Balance

Basically, deciding the appropriate size of an association board involves striking a creative balance. Cyril Houle suggests that a board should be "small enough to act as a deliberative body" and "large enough to carry the necessary responsibilities." In determining an appropriate size for its board, an association should pay special attention to the costs and benefits associated with smaller and larger boards.

Expanding a board's size is a sure way to enrich the board as a human resource, making possible greater diversity in experience, skills, talents, perspectives, and such factors as age, gender, race, and ethnicity. Other purposes served by enlarging board membership include widening the representation of key constituency groups and stakeholder organizations and facilitating the division of governance labor (basically enabling active standing committees).

But larger boards are more difficult to convene and more costly to operate and support. A board of 35 members, for example, can consume a tremendous amount of chief executive time just in the routine keeping-in-touch and care-and-feeding activities. Staff also has to invest considerable time in planning and managing board-related activities. The larger a board gets, the more we must guard against the clear and present danger of a two-tiered board developing: a broader, largely ceremonial board, and a smaller inner-circle board that actually does the governance work.

A small board obviously costs less to operate and is much easier to convene. However, inbreeding and parochialism are dangers to guard against.

Stage of Development

Another factor to be considered in determining the appropriate size of an association board is the stage of an association's development as a nonprofit corporation. The earlier in the life of an association, when staffing is slim and growth a high priority, the more advantageous a larger board will be. A young, rapidly growing association will want the larger board's hands-on assistance and connections to the wider world. A mature, stable association that is well staffed obviously has less need for board members who roll up their sleeves and pitch in to build and grow the association. In other words, when an association is in a strongly entrepreneurial phase, it may need the resources that a larger board brings.

Allocating Board Seats

Associations are all over the ballpark in determining how their boards' seats are allocated. Some reserve seats on their board for particular constituency groups (for example, insurance agents and companies in an association involved in technology research and development in the casualty and property insurance industry; professionals and consumers in an association involved in addressing a medical issue). Others designate seats for election by the membership generally, or by specific subgroups of the membership, and other at-large seats that the board itself fills. And some specifically reserve seats for *outside* board members who are not members of the association as a way of ensuring greater diversity of experience and skills and expanding the association's ties with the wider world.

In addition to the formal identification of types of seats in an association's bylaws, many associations are influenced by informal traditions in allocating board seats. For example, seats may be informally reserved for particular professional types, such as the board's resident legal whiz or financial wizard, or for token representation (our woman, Hispanic, African American).

As with board size, more art than science is involved in determining how board seats will be allocated. The preeminent principle that should govern the determination is:

Does the allocation of our board seats truly promote the best interests of both the association and of its effective governance?

Term Requirements

Also typically covered in an association's bylaws along with board size and types of seats, terms are probably seldom considered as a pressing issue. However, every few years a board should reexamine term requirements to make sure they are meeting the needs of the association and of its governance process. In doing so, it is worth looking at:

Continuity and Growth

Are terms long enough for board members to become skilled at governance work, and are the terms staggered to ensure that turnover does not threaten continuity?

It would be a serious mistake to underestimate the value of experienced members who serve as mentors to newcomers, conveying to them the board's values and traditions and teaching them the tricks of the governance trade. "Long enough" is, of course, a subjective concept, but experience indicates that a term of three-to-four years with the option of reappointment to a second term is sufficient to promote continuity and to enable board members to become expert in the governance business.

New Blood

Too little turnover on an association board can lead to calcification and turn tradition into a vice. The regular infusion of new members onto a board is essential to maintaining a vital governing board that is growing in capability, engaging in healthy questioning of its customs and policies, and keeping up with the ever changing times. Therefore, term limits do make sense, and experience teaches that two consecutive terms of no more than three or four years each will serve well the needs for both continuity and orderly change.

Patterns in Filling Vacancies

Far more important than structural matters such as board size and allocation of seats are the people who actually fill the seats. Indeed, in filling board vacancies an association basically determines the leadership potential and promise of the board, which will be realized through development and implementation of the board's leadership design. Therefore, selecting board members should be treated as a matter of the utmost importance, deserving considerable attention and rigorous management.

Association board members are selected to fill vacancies in various ways. Self-perpetuating boards appoint their own members, with little or no involvement of the membership, while others rely on the board for nomination and the membership for election of new board members. Some associations look to third parties to nominate members for vacancies, and the board itself makes the selections. Numerous variations on these patterns can be found.

Enhancing the Selection Process

However its members are formally selected, an association board can make the process a more powerful board-capability-building vehicle by:

- assigning responsibility for overseeing the board member selection process to a standing committee (see Chapter 7, which suggests that this critical function be assigned to the board's executive committee, rather than to an ad hoc nominating committee)

- ensuring the selection process is guided by a detailed profile of attributes and qualifications (the board member profile) and by more specific current needs of both the board and the association, which should be fashioned by the accountable standing committee and formally adopted by the full board

- systematically identifying likely candidates who meet the general and specific requirements and recruiting them

- keeping the attributes and qualifications updated to reflect changing association needs and circumstances

Progress Despite Constraints

The following discussion of board member nomination and selection is necessarily generic, and the reader must tailor the advice to his or her particular association. In doing so, it is important to keep in mind that, regardless of the constraints in particular situations, the process of filling board seats can be made more effective by applying the following guidelines in some fashion. Let's take, for example, a highly constrained situation, where a board is bound to select new members from a list of nominations submitted by specific membership groups (say, councils organized by geography or industry market segments). As long as it does not violate serious cultural and political norms in the association, the board's executive committee can at least upgrade the selection process by communicating clearly the standards that nominees should meet. Since most association boards are accountable for nominating candidates for board membership, even if they must be elected by the association's membership, the following guidelines can be more easily applied in upgrading the selection process.

Fashioning the Profile

Few, if any, ideal board members who satisfy all of an association's needs and desires are out there to be found, but without a clear, detailed description of the type of board member to use as a guide in the nomination and selection process, an association is far less likely to create the board it needs and wants. The committee responsible for the board member selection process will want to start by fashioning a general profile that identifies the generic attributes and qualifications that the board would like nominees to have. For example, an association board might want prospective new board members to possess:

- an understanding of, and commitment to, the basic mission of the association
- time to devote to full participation on the board and the willingness to commit the time
- experience in nonprofit—and preferably association—governance
- access to political or financial resources
- stature
- a track record of volunteering in the association
- demonstrated ability in, and commitment to, teamwork

Few people possessing all of these attributes and qualifications are likely to be found, but the closer a potential board member comes to fitting the profile, the more attractive his or her candidacy will presumably be. Even when filling seats that have been allocated to particular categories of board members (say, certified professionals in a field or particular constituencies such as clients and customers), priority can be given to the nomination of eligible candidates who most closely fit the general profile.

Judgment Required

It goes without saying that the standards are general and subjective, requiring the board committee (or other body) accountable for identifying likely candidates for board seats to make judgments of the "exactly what/how much is enough" variety. For example, what does stature mean, how is it measured (fame, fortune, professional accomplishments), and how much can the board reasonably expect to get? Chief executive officers of major corporations are obvious candidates, but they are few and far between. Will a corporate vice president of human resources or a chief financial officer do for the association's purposes?

More Specific Qualifications

Of course, the weight given to particular elements of the profile will vary as association and board needs vary. More specific qualifications must often be developed to meet present and anticipated association needs. For example, when a field or industry is going through dramatic restructuring that calls for significant reallocation of resources to new products and services, a board of an association in this field may choose to search for one or more candidates with demonstrated entrepreneurial skills who have extensive experience in planning and launching innovative ventures. In an environment crowded with significant competitors for an association's members and markets, the board may want to identify candidates who represent "friendly" competitors with whom alliances are a possibility. When downsizing and tough choices about where and how much to cut loom on an association's horizon, candidates bringing experience in cost control and contraction management will naturally be attractive.

Membership Diversity

The cultural component of a board's leadership vision can also be important in identifying more specific human resource needs. For example, if a board has identified membership diversity as one of its key values, and its current membership is comprised entirely of white males, it will want to give serious consideration to the identification of candidates who will expand diversity while also possessing to a satisfactory degree the qualifications and attributes of the general profile.

Diversity, which has been touched on briefly in earlier chapters, deserves special attention in light of its significant symbolic and practical benefits, including:

• bringing fresh perspectives and new ideas

- signaling to existing and potential association members a commitment to openness and inclusiveness
- providing an opportunity for members of traditionally underrepresented groups to acquire leadership skills
- attracting association members who might otherwise not be interested

A board is serious about diversifying its membership when it explicitly makes diversity one of its core values and puts its "money" where its mouth is by fashioning and implementing action strategies to achieve greater diversity. Unless coupled with detailed strategy, diversity is most likely a rhetorical objective. For many homogeneous boards, actually diversifying membership can be a real stretch, and some may be tempted to give up the quest prematurely. Serious commitment means going the extra mile to find someone from an underrepresented group even if no likely candidates surface during the initial search.

Beware of the Expertise Trap

It is not uncommon to encounter association boards that have recruited new board members on the basis of the particular expertise they possess. Some have even informally reserved certain seats for particular types of experts, in, for example, the areas of law, finance, financial resource development, public relations, and marketing. An association may view such expertise as a valuable addition to the governance process, bringing important perspectives and skills to decision making. While this may be the case, it is important to keep in mind that the governance mission of a board transcends—and is much more than merely the sum of—such technical specialties. Expertise in law, finance, and any other field does not translate into governance expertise.

To the extent that board members are encouraged to play the role of resident experts, the primary governance mission of a board will suffer. Additionally, resident experts on boards may diminish the sense of collective accountability of the board in key areas. The board as a whole should be accountable for, and knowledgeable about, the financial status of the association, whether or not a standing committee is employed to enhance the board's involvement in finance. Such accountability should never be informally handed to a corporate chief financial officer who happens to serve on the board.

Associations in the infant or adolescent stage of development may be tempted to rely on expert board members to substitute for significant gaps in staff expertise. This use of a board as the supplier of free technical assistance is totally inappropriate, impeding the development and exercise of the board's governance responsibilities while dangerously blurring the distinction between executive management and board governance. As associations employing this approach mature and flesh out their staff capabilities, they are likely to have difficulty in changing their board's focus from executive management to governance. A far better strategy for an association needing expert technical assistance but not able to pay for it is to establish one or more technical advisory committees—bodies of volunteers dedicated to the *nongovernance* function of providing technical assistance.

A Special Strain

A special strain of the expertise virus often infects trade association boards, seriously impeding the development of their governance capability. Associations in highly technical industries (such as those involving computer technology) are especially prone to this infection, since they often see their field as involving such special expertise that only the experts themselves can govern the association. Inevitably dominated by the experts, such boards can easily turn into a kind of grandiose technical advisory committee that tends to become involved in-depth in technical matters at the expense of strong governance.

Identifying Candidates

An association board with direct responsibility for nominating and selecting its own members can employ a number of approaches to identifying likely candidates for board seats—preferably under the leadership of the standing committee responsible for board operations. Since the board's membership is by far its most precious resource and the major determinant of its effectiveness, the search for candidates should be as wide and thorough as possible. And in identifying candidates, the profile of attributes and qualifications should be the major screening device.

One widely practiced technique is to rely on board members themselves to identify candidates they already know, and the more extensive board members' professional networks are, the more fruitful will be this source of candidates. Keep in mind, however, that exclusive reliance on this more personal approach can lead to the kind of inbreeding and parochialism that eats away at a board's leadership capability. An association's membership is another obvious source, and the responsible board committee might also contact key stakeholder organizations in this regard.

Selection

Whether an association board selects its own new members or less directly proposes their selection to a third-party appointer or elector, identified candidates should be recommended only after as thorough a screening as possible. Personal interviewing by the responsible board committee can be a useful screening device, especially if accompanied by the testimony of persons who have had extensive contact with the candidate.

The screening process will be more effective to the extent that it collects and analyzes objective information on a candidate's actual performance and accomplishments in various situations—for example, on other boards—rather than relying exclusively on the more general and subjective testimonials of acquaintances. The committee doing the screening should bear in mind that frequently the likes and dislikes that acquaintances report are based more on style than substance. The fact that a prospective board member may not easily fit into the prevailing culture is just as likely to be an asset as a liability. A spicier stew can be more flavorful and interesting, as long as the new spice does not overwhelm other flavors.

Going for the Prize

If a board has identified a "must" candidate who will fill a particular high-priority niche on the board (say, to tie the association more closely to the funding community), aggressive recruitment is often required. The reason is simple: Highly attractive candidates such as corporate chief executives and philanthropists are typically widely known and sought after by a number of boards. A recruitment strategy that is well conceived and meticulously executed is essential in these instances. Tailoring the strategy to the particular candidate will increase the likelihood of successful pursuit. For example, the presentation of association accomplishments might highlight those apt to tug at the candidate's heartstrings or excite him or her intellectually. Even style can be factored into a strategy. A candidate known to prefer crisp, visual briefings can be treated to a brief slide show that succinctly and attractively gets the key points across.

One technique that has proved very productive is a personal visit by the responsible board committee or one of its members, or by the board chair, perhaps accompanied by the chief executive. A visit will be a far more powerful tool if a formal presentation has been prepared that highlights the association's vision, mission, strategies and accomplishments; describes the board's performance standards and organizational structure; and clearly explains why the candidate is being sought for the board. Is he or she expected to play a specific leadership role (for example, heading a fund-raising committee or chairing the newly formed management committee)? If so, what is the nature of the work involved and how much time will it take? The visiting delegation should expect that the time requirement will be a serious concern and be prepared to address it.

If such a courtship ultimately fails, all is not lost. Highly prized candidates more often than not possess extensive networks and can suggest acquaintances who appear to fit the bill. Also keep in mind that being courted is a pleasing experience that flatters the ego, and that the suitors, despite being spurned, now have a potential friend who can be called on in the future for assistance.

The Celebrity Trap

An association board may be tempted to court a celebrity candidate solely for his or her name on the letterhead, on the assumption that the glory and prestige will rub off on the association. This "look at the company we keep" strategy is vastly overrated and usually causes more harm than good. In the first place, no matter how brightly the celebrity shines, the board and its association will not be illuminated. This strategy has been employed too often to impress any longer. Contemporary audiences know that only a name has been purchased, nothing more, and that it undoubtedly carries little knowledge or commitment with it.

Worse, wooing celebrities for their names alone creates two castes on an association board: the "worker class," whose unillustrious members are expected to toil away in the trenches doing the arduous governance work that must be done if the association is to thrive, and the "leisure class," whose privileged members are too important to make an appearance at all, much less descend into the trench. The message to those toiling away is all too clear.

And finally, the celebrity strategy thoughtlessly fails to use the resource in a creative and productive fashion. We really can do without another name on the board roster. However, a celebrity's chairing a blue-ribbon committee that meets only once every two years for two hours to review association accomplishments and provide advice and counsel on future directions would be a major contribution, as would volunteering to keynote the next annual conference. And if we really cannot get more than a name, there is always the blue-ribbon advisory council that never meets but appears on the letterhead. At least this lowest-common-denominator approach does not violate the board's culture or dilute its governance.

Chapter Six
Managing Board Performance

Once the People Are in Place

Settling such important structural matters as association board size and the allocation of board seats and ensuring that the right people are found to fill the seats are essential steps in the direction of strong board leadership. However, whether the assembled cast works well together, making the whole truly more productive than the sum of its parts, is another matter entirely. This chapter focuses on two strategies that an association board can employ to realize its full leadership potential:

- consciously and systematically managing its own performance as a governing body
- developing its members' capability to carry out their challenging governance responsibilities

Board Accountability

There is good reason to believe that many, if not most, association boards do not take collective, formal accountability for the performance of their governance work and, hence, do not attempt to develop any kind of board performance management system. The still-common passive model of board leadership, which sees the board as the apex of the association pyramid, does not pay much attention to managing board performance. Traditionally, boards and chief executives have just not seen anything much worth managing.

Of course, the very opposite is true. Boards do the very important—indeed, preeminent—governance work of their associations, and if they do not manage this work explicitly and systematically, the odds will be against its being well done. No one else can take accountability for the board's performance; certainly only a masochistic chief executive with a strong death wish would try. John Carver puts it well:

Board members, not staff, are morally trustees for the ownership and, consequently, must bear initial responsibility for the integrity of governance. The board is responsible for its own development, its own job design, its own discipline, and its own performance. Before any discussion of board process to improve governance, this responsibility must be clear to board and staff alike.

Overcoming Reluctance

Board performance management involves doing two critical jobs: setting clear board performance standards and monitoring performance, taking corrective action as appropriate. Before looking at each of these jobs in detail, the reader should keep in mind that they cannot be done fully and well unless the whole board takes formal, collective responsibility for doing them. Board members are naturally reluctant to criticize, or even comment on, each other's performance. Life is short and challenging enough as it is, without alienating colleagues with whom we must spend time. Even the board chair is doomed to fail if he or she attempts to become the czar of board performance; such a perceived "power grab" would inevitably result in the gavel's being passed to a less presumptuous leader.

The principle of collective accountability for performance will not be violated if a standing committee is given responsibility for doing the detailed performance management work and for overseeing the operation of the process. The committee already accountable for overseeing the board member nomination and selection process would be a sensible candidate for the performance management responsibility (see Chapter 7 for a detailed discussion of standing committees).

The Chief Executive's Role

No association chief executive in his or her right mind would dare to take the lead in establishing board performance standards or in assessing the board's performance. But as an integral member of the association leadership team, the chief executive must play an important role in the performance management process. Indeed, the chief executive has no choice but to play an assertive role in board performance management, for two important reasons. First, an association board that does not build a strong board performance management process will function less effectively, consequently feel less satisfied, and typically hold the poor chief executive accountable for its frustration. Second, only the chief executive has the time and other resources that are essential for carrying out the performance management process.

Rather than taking formal accountability and leading the board performance management process, a savvy chief executive will lead from behind, working as a facilitator and supporter. For example, opportunities for creative contribution include:

- working closely with the board chair in building board members' commitment to managing their own performance (This may very likely require a front-end information and education strategy, aimed at making board members aware of the importance of self-management and acquainting them with examples of successful practice. For example, both the American Society of Association Executives and the National Center for

Nonprofit Boards have published helpful pieces on board performance management that are intended for busy board members. Obtaining the formal commitment to engage in systematic self-management may require a board-staff retreat, at which this complex matter can be explored in detail.)

- actively assisting in designing and implementing the board performance management process, working closely with the responsible board committee to fashion performance standards and to put in place a process for monitoring performance.

- providing the support required to carry out the monitoring process, making sure that meetings of the responsible committee are scheduled, that agendas are well crafted, required information is available on time, and committee actions are followed up on

Setting Performance Standards

Performance standards address both what board members are expected to do (work content) and the values that will govern their behavior and interactions with each other as they go about doing their governance work (the board's culture). The development of the board leadership design that is described in Chapter 3 will supply much of the information to answer the two questions. These standards should be formally codified in a detailed policy statement that the board adopts, for the purpose of providing the yardstick by which the performance of board members can be gauged.

Association boards involved in managing their own performance have established job content standards relating to:

- attendance at board meetings (How many absences are allowable, and what excuses are acceptable?)
- preparation for, and participation in, board meetings
- service on standing committees (What attendance standards apply here, and how can the quality of participation be gauged?)
- participation in special board work sessions
- financial support (Are board members expected to contribute financially to the association, and if so, what is the minimum acceptable contribution?)
- external relations (Are board members expected to build the association's image and public relations by speaking on its behalf in appropriate forums? If so, how often and in what forums, and how will the members' performance be evaluated?)

Values that comprise a board's internal culture and regulate the behavior of its members address such matters as how potential or actual conflicts of interest are to be handled, how board members are to communicate with the chief executive and staff members, how matters will be brought to the attention of the board, how information will be shared, how communication on behalf of the board with the wider public will be handled, and what standards are to govern board members' interactions with each other (for example, to employ no hidden agendas; to treat each other civilly in meetings, no matter how heated discussion might become; not to question board decisions publicly after the vote has been taken).

Meaning Through Enforcement

If a standing committee is responsible for monitoring board members' performance and for taking appropriate steps to address shortfalls, the process has a much better chance of working. The real challenge is not to set the standards, but to give them meaning through enforcement. A number of technical questions need to be answered in this regard. For example, the responsible committee needs to determine what information to collect and how and when to collect it so that it can keep track of performance.

But the real challenge is to overcome the natural resistance of volunteers to evaluating each other's performance, and to a lesser extent having their own performance monitored. For most governance volunteers, initiating a formal performance management process will be a dramatic break with the past that must be introduced with great care.

Approaches to Consider

Enforcement needs to be thought through in detail before launching a board performance management process. Shortfalls in performance must have consequences if the process is to have any credibility, but the ultimate penalty—being asked to resign or being removed by board action—should truly be a last resort. The responsible committee must develop a clear, graduated sequence of actions, moving from merely alerting an errant board member to his or her performance deficiency (say, having missed two consecutive planning committee meetings); to counseling and assistance in remedying performance; to direr warnings; and, only after all else has proved fruitless, letting the proverbial axe fall.

The performance management process is apt to break down if it is perceived as insensitive or needlessly punitive. The governing principles in enforcing performance should be:

- retaining every board member if humanly possible
- making every effort to assist board members in improving lagging performance
- avoiding any public embarrassment of board members whose performance deficiencies have been flagged
- providing ample warning before any step in the process is taken

Building Members' Capability

Low-Cost/High-Yield Steps

Fashioning a detailed board leadership design that spells out board products, roles, structure, and process and launching a serious board performance management process are dramatic steps and substantial investments that will yield tremendous, enduring returns. But association boards can engage in a number of less dramatic and less costly activities that will build the leadership capability of their members.

Provide a Comprehensive, Formal Orientation.

Many association board members can recall their confusion and discomfort in the early days of their governance tenure, as they merely jumped into the fray with virtually no preparation or guidance. Concentrating on trying not to look as inept as they felt and keeping quiet about complex issues not fully understood, they slowly but surely learned the ropes and began to contribute to the deliberations. What a waste of precious volunteer time—time that their associations truly needed.

A sure-fire way to bring new board members up to speed sooner, to reap benefits from their participation earlier, and to avoid their early disillusionment is to provide a formal orientation program that describes in detail the association's history, current vision, mission, and strategic directions; the association's major functions and organizational chart; the board's leadership design—its major products, structure, and processes; and board performance standards. Merely handing new board members an ugly blob of paper will not suffice. The orientation should include both an attractive, easy-to-read notebook conveying the pertinent information and a session with the board chair and chief executive officer.

Assign an Experienced Board Member as Mentor.

Learning the governance ropes will be a much easier and enjoyable process if, in addition to the orientation, every new board member is mentored by an experienced board member, who will make sure that his or her charge fully understands how the board operates and grasps the critical issues currently facing the board. One of the mentor's most important functions is to answer the new member's "stupid" questions that typically go unasked.

Provide Opportunities for Education and Training.

The best way to learn is by doing, rather than being preached to, and so actually participating in carrying out a board leadership design is the ultimate form of education and training in governance. However, governance skills can certainly be expanded and honed by participation in conferences and training workshops. Two ingredients will ensure that the process yields a strong return in strengthened capability: first, by making a standing committee responsible for establishing education and training priorities, identifying and selecting opportunities, and assessing the results; second, by establishing a budget to pay the costs of conference and workshop attendance.

Regularly Share Important Information.

This is a time of exciting change in nonprofit management generally and in related subfields such as governance, chief executiveship, and strategic planning. At the very least, board members can be kept apprised of major developments pertinent to their leadership responsibilities, by drawing to their attention (and sometimes purchasing for their reading pleasure) books and monographs and by circulating copies of articles. An association library that subscribes to relevant publications and purchases pertinent new books would be a valuable resource to the board.

Chief Executive Role

The chief executive officer has a critical facilitative and supportive role to play in board members' capability building. For one thing, he or she can take the time to track advances in nonprofit and association management and regularly communicate them to the board, through both oral reports at board meetings and in periodical bulletins. The chief executive can also bring professional development opportunities, such as workshops and conferences, to the board's attention. Membership in such organizations as the American Society of Association Executives, the National Center for Nonprofit Boards, and the Society for Nonprofit Organizations, to name but a few, will expand the chief executive's knowledge of educational opportunities.

An association chief executive who is strongly committed to board capability building can also spend time educating himself or herself in the human growth process, delving into recent work in such areas as human learning, creativity, innovation, and team building (see Chapter 14). Armed with the most recent knowledge, a committed chief executive can put his or her mind to work, figuring out how this learning can be translated into practical board capability building. One obvious way is to ensure that board retreats are designed and conducted with this knowledge in mind.

A Never-Ending Journey

Developing the board as a human resource is a journey with no final destination. Some segments are traveled together as a board, others as individual board members. Human growth has no natural limits, at least none we have come close to reaching, and so capability building has plenty of room for expansion. How far a board chooses to travel along the road of human development and growth, and how fast, will have a tremendous impact on the board's performance of its governance work. For, as was noted at the beginning of Chapter 5, boards are basically people, and bringing their talents, skills, experiences, and perspectives fully to bear in addressing governance matters is the most powerful tool at our command for strengthening board leadership.

In the next two chapters, I look at a number of important structural matters, most notably board committee structure, and that preeminent alliance for progress, the board-chief executive officer partnership.

Chapter Seven
More on Structure

Organizing to Govern

Structure relates to how an association board organizes to carry out its governance role and leadership processes. The most important structural questions, such as board member nomination and selection, terms, standing committees, and meeting requirements, are spelled out in an association's bylaws. Chapter 5 addresses the human resource dimension of structure in some detail. In this chapter I look at standing committees, the board chair's role, how to resolve the confusion between governance and other volunteering in volunteer-driven associations, and meeting schedules.

Surprisingly Passionate

Although at first blush structural questions such as committee structure appear exceedingly dry and straightforward, they tend to generate a surprising amount of heat. Many people are quite capable of feeling more passionate about whether to have standing committees than about such exalted matters as vision and mission. And in the throes of such passion, advocates of one position or another are, when challenged, all too ready to man the ramparts and fight to the death for their cause.

Guiding Principle

I would like to propose an overarching principle that might, in lieu of a real science of board structure, help to cut through preconceived notions and pet solutions:

The best structural approaches are those that

- contribute most directly and powerfully to the achievement of a board's leadership mission
- are affordable in the sense that they can be implemented within a reasonable time without overtaxing an association's resources

If this broad principle is the guiding force in addressing board structural questions, then whether someone has become romantically attached to a particular committee type (a mild and curable neurosis) is beside the point. What works best for board governance is what counts.

Why Have Committees?

Few people appear to be neutral on the subject of committees. Some people truly hate them, others believe they should always be ad hoc, serving a specific purpose and then disbanding, while many accept them as a useful device for getting work done. The fact is, standing committees can serve a number of useful purposes for association boards. They can foster:

Productivity—They enable an association board to get more governance work done by dividing the labor.

Depth—They also enable a board to get into governance matters in greater depth, which can not only provide a more interesting and enjoyable experience, but also promote greater board impact, thereby providing board members with the satisfaction that comes from making a difference.

Resource Utilization—They make it possible to tap more fully the resources that board members bring to their work—their experience, expertise, talents, and networks—by matching board members carefully with committee assignments.

Capability Building—They facilitate the acquisition of expertise and special skills that can enhance a board's leadership capability.

Board-Staff Interaction—They provide a nonthreatening venue for creative, open, board-staff interaction.

Bad Worse Than None

Underperforming or malfunctioning committees can erode the credibility of an association board and weaken the commitment of its members to the governance function. It would almost certainly be better for a board to have no committees than to have a weak structure that does not function effectively. Countless times, I have listened to the frustration of association board members who serve on committees that have not met for several months, or hold somewhat aimless discussion sessions, leaving them puzzled and often disaffected.

Organizing Along Governance Lines

Successful board committees that contribute significantly to the governance process are organized along *broad governance lines*, directly relating to the actual work of the board, rather than along administrative or programmatic lines. If an association board is structured along programmatic lines (for example, a chamber of commerce with a downtown business district committee or a business attraction and retention committee), the liabilities are obvious. The board will:

Find it Difficult to Provide Associationwide Direction—It will be extremely difficult for a board with such committees to provide the cross-cutting, associationwide direction that is the basic purpose of governance.

Promote Advocacy and Dabbling—Focusing on particular components of an association's business, rather than on governance matters, will promote two negative traits among board members: *Advocacy* for particular programs and *dabbling* in program management.

Underutilize Members—Board members, as a human resource, will be used at a lower level—basically as *technical advisers*, rather than as *governors*, not only reducing their impact, but also eroding their interest, enthusiasm, and commitment over time.

A Model Structure

An association board's committee structure that directly contributes to carrying out its governance work might include three broadly functional standing committees (see Figure 5):

Planning and Program Development—responsible for working closely with the chief executive officer in the design of an annual planning and program development process that will involve the board at key points—proactively and creatively. This committee provides hands-on guidance in developing the strategic framework (vision, mission, broad directions, selection of strategic issues) and in preparing the annual operational plan and budget. It takes the lead in planning—and hosts—any intensive board-staff planning work sessions.

Operations—responsible for working closely with the chief executive in the design and implementation of a programmatic and fiscal performance monitoring process that involves the board in a meaningful fashion. It reviews performance reports in-depth and reports both progress and problems to the full board.

Membership and External Relations—responsible for working closely with the chief executive in setting directions and monitoring performance in the areas of membership development and relations, image building, and public relations. This committee is responsible for working out in detail hands-on board responsibilities in external relations, such as speaking on behalf of the association or serving as liaison with particular stakeholders.

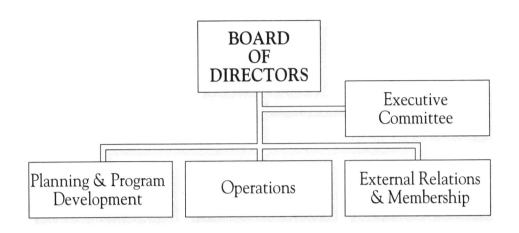

Figure 5. Model Committee Structure

Not Too Many

The foregoing structure clearly mirrors an association board's major governance responsibilities. It is also attractive because it involves only three committees. Experience has taught that a "critical mass" of board members is necessary for a committee to be very productive; at least five members are preferable to ensure diverse skills, perspectives, and experience. Up to ten members, or even fifteen, can be accommodated on a committee, so long as its meetings are meticulously planned, supported, and facilitated. Keeping to three—or perhaps four committees at the most—also has the powerful advantage of grouping closely related governance functions. For example, the planning and program development committee deals not only with strategic planning, but also operational planning and budget preparation. The operations committee handles both programmatic and fiscal monitoring, while external relations groups such similar functions as public information, marketing, membership relations, and stakeholder management.

Creative Board-Chief Executive Interaction

Some association chief executives might feel threatened by the prospect of strong standing committees that actually become involved in designing the processes in which they participate (such as strategic and operational planning or fiscal and program performance management). Rather than reacting defensively, chief executives should see such committees as an ideal venue for exploring creatively the board-chief executive division of labor, vis a vis the association's most important leadership processes. By explicitly deciding how performance management will be handled, for example, and precisely how the board and chief executive will work together in monitoring performance, the potential for unfulfilled expectations and conflict will be significantly reduced.

Take, for example, an association's strategic and operational planning cycle. Planning has in recent years evolved in new directions that offer opportunities for more creative board involvement (See Chapter 9 for a detailed discussion of the planning function). Traditionally, nonprofit boards have rightly found their participation in the planning process to be passive, reactive, and relatively unimportant. So, the savvy association executive has an excellent opportunity—wearing his or her facilitator "hat"—to work closely with the board in both updating how their association will do planning and ensuring that the board plays a strong and creative role in the process. There are no right or wrong answers in dividing up the action and the labor involved in planning; only through detailed dialogue between a board and its chief executive can the appropriate roles be determined. A standing committee focused on planning is an ideal vehicle for working through the division of labor and defining the roles. And because the committee setting is more relaxed than a full board meeting, such questions can be worked through without the drama and potential for losing face that can make full board meetings tense affairs.

Making Committees Work Well

The following simple guidelines will help to ensure the productivity of an association board's standing committees.

Only Board Members—Board members should comprise the standing committees because they—and they only—are charged to govern. Of course, executive team members should attend, and should participate actively, but they are not governors. In addition, association volunteers not on the board can be enlisted to serve on special task forces and technical advisory groups under the appropriate committees.

All Board Members but the Chair—If standing committees are to be a major governance "engine" of the board, all board members but the board chair should be required to serve and their performance as committee members should be monitored (see Chapter 6).

Only One Committee Assignment—Board members are extremely busy people whose time is scarce and precious; to expect them to contribute at a high level in more than one committee is unrealistic.

Careful Chair and Member Selection—Strong committee chairs are essential for committee productivity, and traits that contribute to strength in this critical role are: passion for the subject matter of the committee (some people are clearly planning enthusiasts, others love number crunching); the willingness to commit the time required; pertinent experience and expertise; respect of peers; strong organizing, and group process skills. In addition, board members' expressed preferences, demonstrated skill and competence, and experience should be considered in making committee assignments.

Clear Charge and Detailed Orientation—Nothing kills credibility quicker than a fumbling start, and providing committee members with a clear, detailed description of their responsibilities as part of a comprehensive orientation on committee work will help to ensure committee productivity.

Empowerment—Board members expect to contribute in powerful ways to the affairs of their association, and they do not have time for discussion groups. A simple step can empower a board's standing committees: *Require that every agenda item at full board meetings has passed through one of the standing committees, all board actions are introduced by committees, and all reports (other than the board chair's and CEO's) are made by committee members, including the financial report.*

Strong Staff Support—Assigning one or more staff members to work with particular committees will help to make them effective. Staff can assist in preparing agendas, developing needed documentation, contributing to discussion, and preparing committee reports to the board.

The Debate Over Executive Committees

In the committee business, there is probably a no more heatedly debated subject than whether to have an executive committee. They have earned their bad rap without question. In too many instances, executive committees have become "petite" boards within the larger board, elite bodies that actually do the work of the larger board, which exists only to confirm their actions. When this is allowed to happen, the value of service on the full board declines and the ill winds of resentment, suspicion, and sometimes even paranoia begin to blow.

An executive committee can be a sensible mechanism for securing board approval of an action in a true emergency situation, which is a far cry from routinely serving as a little board within the board. But the most compelling reason for an executive committee is *to serve as the committee on board operations, directing and coordinating the work of the board.*

If the executive committee does its job well, the board is able to perform its governance work more effectively and efficiently.

Headed by the board chair and preferably consisting of the standing committee chairs, the executive committee might:

- oversee the functioning of the association board, which might involve directing and coordinating the work of the standing committees, establishing board members' performance standards, monitoring members' performance, and recommending action to the board in instances of performance inadequacies
- negotiate annual performance targets with the association's chief executive officer and evaluate his or her performance at least annually (see Chapter 8 for a detailed discussion of chief executive evaluation)

- carry out the board membership renewal function, developing desired board member qualifications and attributes (a profile), identifying likely candidates for board vacancies, fashioning and executing strategies to attract new board members, and identifying and recommending the appointment of new members (see Chapter 5 for a close look at board membership development)

- ensure that a comprehensive orientation program for new board members is developed and implemented and that the leadership capability of members is systematically developed (see Chapter 6).

Transition Takes Time

New standing committees typically do not "hit the ground running." To expect them to become fully productive soon after their initiation will be unrealistic. For one thing, few if any members of, say, the new planning committee, are likely to have served in exactly this role in an association. Very likely, they have participated in traditional program-focused committees that have involved them in reacting to finished staff work. Therefore, patience is very much in order. The reader should assume that 12 to 18 months might be required for a new committee to hit its stride. One step that can help a new committee get started is to hold a kick-off planning and organization session, at which the new committee:

- develops its "production" priorities for the coming year, specifying what its major accomplishments will be—for example, a newly established operations committee may target the development of a new financial reporting process for its initial year

- maps out a committee workplan to achieve the targets, spelling out committee and staff roles and responsibilities

- decides how the committee will operate, including how often it will meet, the format for its reports, how it wants staff to participate, and so forth

And remember, new committees cannot simply replace existing ones in one fell swoop fashion. Very often, existing committees are in the midst of doing work that cannot merely be dropped, or picked up by a new committee. It will always make sense, therefore, to develop a detailed transition plan that provides for the orderly phasing in and out of committees so as to ensure that nothing important falls through the proverbial cracks.

Role of Board Chairs

There is considerable confusion and debate about the appropriate role of association board chairs in the affairs of the association. Some association board chairs are also chief elected officials of their association, usually with the title "president" as well as board chair. In these instances, the full-time, paid professional who serves as the association's chief executive officer is typically given the title "executive director." But in some associations, the full-time top professional is given the title "president and chief executive officer," and the volunteer who heads the board is simply the "board chair."

Some Simple Guidelines

What really matters in practice is not titles, but roles, responsibilities, and working relationships. In this regard, the following straightforward guidelines may help both association board chairs and their chief executive officers to keep their sanity.

1. Every association must have a full-time, paid professional to carry out the chief executive officer role. This professional, whether titled "president" or "executive director" is appointed by the board, evaluated by the board, and reports only to the board.

2. Every association board must be headed by a part-time, unpaid volunteer who is typically called the board "chair." This volunteer's preeminent job is to lead the board, ensuring that it does its job in a full and timely fashion. He or she chairs the executive committee.

3. When an unpaid association volunteer who chairs the association's board is also the elected "president" of the association, this usually means that he or she takes on a larger ceremonial role (for example, chairing annual membership meetings) and perhaps a significant diplomatic role, speaking for the association in a variety of public forums.

4. Under no circumstances should the volunteer who chairs the board and serves as the chief elected official of the association take on any internal chief executive officer functions. *The chief executive officer role is not divided where internal planning and management responsibilities are concerned.*

5. However, the board chair and chief executive officer should collaborate closely in the external affairs arena, explicitly dividing the external representation responsibilities and on occasion appearing on platforms together (say, at legislative hearings or on a television talk show).

6. Although the board chair and chief executive officer should develop a close working partnership, especially where board operations and external relations are concerned, the chief executive should take direction only from the board collectively and never from the board chair as an individual. Nor is it ever appropriate for the chief executive to negotiate his or her performance targets with the board chair or to be evaluated by the chair.

Effective Board Chairs

What do we know about effective board chairs? First and foremost, they are passionately committed to strong board leadership. They view their most important role as ensuring that their board functions as a top-notch governance body. They also tend to be more effective in their board leadership role if they bring extensive governance experience to the boardroom, along with a generous dollop of vision and strong facilitative skills. And, of course, board chairs who put any personal agendas they may have well behind the overall welfare of the whole association and well below the operation of the board will be more effective in leading an association board.

Untangling Volunteering

America's tradition of volunteer-led and driven associations is alive and sometimes well, almost entirely among smaller associations at the local level. Examples are chambers of commerce and women's groups such as sections of the National Council of Jewish Women and the Women's City Clubs in New York City and Cleveland. Typically, the volunteer-driven organization:

- is very slimly staffed; indeed, it often has only a part-time executive who may function more as an administrative assistant than a chief executive
- depends on part-time, unpaid volunteers to play a hands-on role well beyond governing— in developing and running programs and in carrying out a wide variety of administrative duties, ranging from keeping the books and preparing financial reports to stuffing envelopes
- uses volunteer involvement in program and administrative operations as both a major qualification for, and a kind of career ladder to, governance board service
- very often expects that its board members continue to participate heavily in nonboard volunteering, as a condition of "employment" in governance.

Major Challenges

Local volunteer-driven associations that fit this profile are running into some serious problems that, for some, jeopardize their effectiveness and even threaten their very existence. In a time of accelerating change, including the virtual disappearance of the professional volunteer whose only job is contributing time to worthwhile causes, developing strong leadership, planning, and management capability is a pressing need. However, volunteer-driven associations have tended not to develop the structures and processes required, nor, of course, to staff them with professionals.

The most serious challenge is in association governance. In the first place, strong governance structures and processes have typically not developed in an environment of heavy hands-on volunteering in operational matters. For example, it is common to find board "vice-presidents" who head committees that have nothing to do with broad governance responsibilities, but, rather, oversee particular program areas. A chamber of commerce, for example, might have a governmental affairs committee or a downtown development committee.

Such operational committees tend, naturally, to become strong advocates for their particular programs, and so board meetings easily become merely listening and confirming forums. In the absence of a planning committee that oversees a well-developed planning process, decisions involving the allocation of resources among programs tend to become overly political, driven more by the persuasive talents of vice presidents and advocates than by overall association interests.

And the expectation—or even requirement—that board members of such volunteer-driven associations will remain actively involved in nongovernance, hands-on volunteering virtually assures that a stronger governance process will not be developed. There is just not the time or energy to devote to designing, much less carrying out, a contemporary governance role.

Resolving the Dilemma

Four steps, simple in concept, can resolve this critical dilemma for volunteer-driven associations:

1. **Separate Governance from Other Volunteering**—First, clearly distinguish between volunteering to govern an association through serving on its board and all other kinds of nonboard volunteering.

2. **Focus Board Members on Governance**—Second, require that board members spend all of their volunteer time on governance and do not expect or demand any other kind of volunteering in the association.

3. **Do Away with the Career Ladder Approach**—Third, abolish the career ladder approach to board member selection and appointment. Successful volunteering outside of the board is only one of a number of qualifications to be considered, and very likely not one of the most pertinent.

4. **Establish Governance Committees**—Fourth, establish true governance—rather than operational—committees whose work is associationwide, transcending and cutting across all programs and activities, and whose advocacy is only for the whole association.

Untangle, Not Dismantle

Strengthening the governance structure and process of a volunteer-driven association will involve change, but it need not occur at the expense of other volunteering, nor should it tarnish the luster of volunteerism as a guiding value. Nongovernance volunteer committees engaged in program operations need not be eliminated as part of upgrading governance, but they must be *uncoupled* from an association's board. The myth that they contribute to governance should disappear, and true governance committees should be established.

Now, in practice, we recognize that volunteering can take many valuable forms, all equal in importance. We can volunteer to be program managers, we can volunteer to do administrative tasks, or we can volunteer to govern by serving on the board. The types of volunteering are distinct, and one does not naturally flow to another.

Although this uncoupling process makes the best of sense and seems relatively simple in concept, some resistance should be expected. Long-tenured board members who have successfully climbed the association career ladder to the board may feel threatened. If not handled sensitively, such reform may appear to be an all-out assault on the culture of volunteerism.

A Word on Meeting Schedules

There is no "right" meeting schedule for boards and their standing committees. The decision should take into account both the needs of association governance and of the individuals comprising the board. Strong, fully engaged, standing committees, a committed and supportive chief executive officer, and the active assistance of staff can help a full board to accomplish its oversight role in two to four meetings annually.

Local association boards often fall into the trap of monthly full board meetings, which make serious committee work well nigh impossible and chew up tremendous time with little important governance impact. Boards that meet this often tend to function as operational committees of the whole, with lots of briefing and discussing, but not much serious decision making. Quarterly meetings almost always suffice when standing committees are doing their job fully.

Chapter Eight
The Board-Executive Partnership

Boards Cannot Go It Alone

No matter how well designed, talented and committed its membership, no association board can fully develop its leadership capability or effectively exercise its governance responsibilities. Volunteers devote only a small part of their lives to board business; always claiming the lion's share of attention are their families and full-time professional obligations. So a board that intends to provide strong, proactive leadership must rely on the support of an *executive infrastructure* consisting of:

- a chief executive officer who is committed to effective governance and backs up his or her words with concrete assistance that facilitates board leadership
- an executive team that is collectively involved in supporting board performance
- well-developed planning and management systems whose design offers significant opportunities for the exercise of board influence and the generation of pertinent information for board decision making

Preeminent Alliance for Progress

An association's board and chief executive officer are its preeminent alliance for progress. If the working partnership between these key members of the nuclear leadership family malfunctions in any significant way, an association can pay a high price. Tension will be the least of the costs. Far more important than unpleasantness, progress toward realizing the association's vision can be slowed, as exciting opportunities are missed and problems go unaddressed. Fulfillment of its mission can be stymied as program operations are disrupted. And once the wider public gets wind of trouble in an association's nuclear family, political and financial support can drastically shrink. When the consequences appear dire enough, association boards usually resolve such troubled relationships by sending their chief executives packing; boards are not known to assign themselves blame, much less to fire themselves. While simple and momentarily satisfying, such a parting of company misses the point, more often than not, and it can be quite costly in terms of negative publicity and internal disruption. There are surely occasions when a board has misjudged in choosing a chief executive whose capabilities are truly not up to the job. The only sensible course, then, is to cut the association's losses and start over with a new chief executive. However, the truth of the situation is usually more complex.

Getting Off to a Good Start

The reader knows from experience that such dramatic and costly partings are likely to be less the result of inadequate chief executive capability, or even of poor performance, than of inadequate board-chief executive relationship building. The odds of a board-chief executive partnership's succeeding over the long run are much greater if: (1) the board's recruitment and selection process is thoughtful and methodical; (2) reciprocal expectations and obligations are made explicit at the onset; (3) the board regularly conducts outcomes-based evaluation of chief executive performance; and (4) the chief executive officer is committed to developing the skills and style that contribute to a positive and productive working relationship.

Selecting a Chief Executive Officer

The key to successful recruitment and selection of a chief executive officer is an association board's identifying in detail what the association needs now and in the next few years in terms of chief executive leadership, and communicating these expectations clearly to applicants. There are, of course, the core competencies good for all times and places, such as demonstrated skills and experience in: supporting and working with nonprofit (and preferably association) boards; designing and carrying out effective strategic and operational planning processes and modern management systems; financial planning and management; team management and team building; external relations, including partnership building and public speaking.

Naturally, an association board will not want to consider seriously any candidate who cannot provide solid evidence of at least minimum capability in each of these core competencies. If a candidate has in the past proved to be terribly uncomfortable speaking in pubic, unable to work successfully in a team setting, or easily "snowed" by accountants, he or she is probably too great a risk to bet on. However, no candidate for the chief executive's job is likely to possess equal experience and skill in every aspect of the job; nor is every one of the requirements equally important at any given time to the association. The selection process will be much more powerful if an association board's thinking about the chief executive job goes beyond the bare minimum, routine requirements.

Tailoring Requirements

In fleshing out a more powerful chief executive requirements statement, an association board will want to start with the association's evolving vision, mission, and any strategic initiatives that have been launched. It will want to reflect on the challenges and opportunities that the association is likely to face in its changing environment, and on internal organizational development priorities in light of serious weaknesses that have been identified. This more searching analysis will enable the board to define extraordinary attributes and qualifications closely tailored to the association's highest priority needs that go beyond normal chief-executive functions.

For example, take an association whose members' needs are changing dramatically, calling into question existing services and products. Membership has, as a result, stopped growing and is perhaps on the downswing. The health care field, now in the midst of radical restructuring, would provide many such examples. In this situation, an association board will want to find a candidate for the chief executive officer position who has an entrepreneurial bent and large-scale experience in successfully developing and launching new products and in stimulating organizational growth.

But if an association's challenge is the control and management—rather than stimulation—of rapid growth, the preeminent need may well be to develop a management infrastructure capable of bringing order and discipline to operations. This association's board will be more interested in a candidate who brings significant skills and experience in designing and implementing sophisticated management systems. And if a rotten internal culture—the result of years of tyrannical leadership in the Marquis de Sade mode—is the largest obstacle in the way of association growth, then the board will want to find evidence of exceptional human resource development and team building skills.

Trade-Offs

An association board looking for a chief executive with extraordinary skills and experience in a particular area, such as launching new products, should keep in mind that no candidate for the job is likely to possess extraordinary qualifications in other areas as well, and may, indeed, be relatively weak in some. The fact is, entrepreneurial types who thrive on invention and the management of change are likely to have less passion for—and less capability in—systems design and internal nuts and bolts management. It would be wishful thinking to expect equal passion and skill in every area of chief executiveship, and so a board must be willing to trade off exceptional qualifications in one area for less in another.

Expectations and Obligations

Selecting the right person for an association's most important job is no small feat, but far more is involved in building and sustaining a productive, mutually satisfying board-chief executive partnership than merely filling the position. The next step is for the board and its new chief executive to reach detailed agreement on the:

- chief executive's performance targets for the coming year
- board commitments required to enable the chief executive to achieve the targets
- rules that are to govern board-chief executive interaction
- process that will be followed to assess chief executive performance

An Annual Affair

The board-chief executive negotiation of targets, commitments, and relationship rules—too important to be dealt with perfunctorily—goes well beyond the typical functional job description. It should become an annual affair, probably best held shortly before the beginning of a new fiscal year and after the board and executive team have reached agreement on the coming year's operational plan (operating unit targets and budgets). The board, or at least its executive committee, should set aside a half-day in a setting free of distractions for this purpose. While it would be helpful for the chief executive to come to the session having prepared formal recommendations relative to performance targets and board commitments, the primary intent of the session is to reach explicit agreement on the basis of in-depth dialogue. A board's merely signing off on a chief executive's thoughts would miss the point entirely.

Performance Promises

There are two tiers of chief executive performance. As the top staff person in the association, the chief executive is without question accountable to the board in general for the achievement of the association's operating targets, as set forth in the annual operational plan and budget, and for maintaining fiscal stability by keeping revenues and expenditures in balance. But the contract between an association board and its chief executive officer is not complete without agreement on the chief executive's *individual* performance targets, above and beyond the formal plan and budget. These individual targets are the primary subject of the chief executive's annual negotiation with the board or its executive committee.

External Relations

The annual negotiation session can be facilitated by dividing chief executive performance into three broad categories: external relations, board support, and internal planning and management. The point is for the board and its chief executive to reach detailed agreement on the individual priorities and contributions of the chief executive in each of these areas. For example, in the external relations arena, a board and chief executive might agree that he or she should focus considerable personal attention over the coming year to laying the foundation for an eventual merger with a sister association, visiting every one of the regional offices at least twice, or increasing membership among an extremely promising, but hard-to-reach segment of the market.

Board Support

In the realm of board support, a chief executive might promise to implement a new performance reporting system intended to give the board a much stronger handle on association progress and problems vis a vis clear performance targets, or to ensure that the board's new standing committee structure is fully implemented within six months.

Internal Planning and Management

Turning to internal planning and management, a chief executive might promise to spend at least 25 percent of her time ensuring that a new automated financial management system is implemented, or that strategies to address serious staff morale problems are carried out.

Means Can Be Important

Although performance targets are essentially outcomes and the focus of evaluation should be the achievement of these ends rather than how they are to be achieved, there are times when the means are important enough to be specified during the negotiation of targets; they should subsequently be monitored and evaluated by the board. For example, if an association has gone through a long period of instability, during which some staff have been laid off and the survivors have been under tremendous stress for months, how a new chief executive goes about making certain changes will be tremendously important. In this instance, any changes made should be carefully paced so as not to add undue stress and should be carried out with sensitivity. The last thing either the board or its new chief executive needs is to add the proverbial straw to an already overloaded camel's back.

Board Promises

Now, if an association chief executive is willing to make a commitment to specific individual accomplishments for the coming year, in addition to accountability for overall association performance, it behooves the board to provide the support that is required for chief executive success. In this regard, the board should:

Allow Tradeoffs—Chief-executive time and energy are a precious and finite resource. Increased time and attention in one area inevitably comes at the expense of another. In fairness to its chief executive, an association board should be willing to negotiate such trade-offs, allowing, for example, less chief executive attention to internal operations, in exchange for intensive chief executive involvement in merger diplomacy. One caveat, however: A chief executive's responsibility in negotiating such trade-offs is to spell out for the board the possible costs and risks involved, so that the board's decisions are truly informed and that the association is not put in jeopardy because of reduced chief executive attention to a critical aspect of association operations. Furthermore, the chief executive should identify the resources needed to avert possible problems, such as allotting one-third of a senior staff member's time to the uncovered area on an interim basis, until the chief executive can refocus his or her attention.

Commit Resources—Of course, chief executive time and attention may not, alone, be sufficient to tackle a performance target. Consider the chief executive who commits to building a modern financial management system for the association that will, once and for all, make it possible to do sophisticated financial forecasting, program cost accounting, and reliable, easy-to-understand financial reporting. The board may need to provide funding for consulting assistance, software acquisition, and the hiring of a chief financial officer. Or, if a board wants the chief executive to concentrate on external relations and financial resource development, it may need to fund a new chief internal operating officer to oversee all program and administrative operations, freeing the chief executive to concentrate on, and hence succeed in, the external role.

Annual Negotiation of Targets

Annual board-chief executive negotiation of targets is essential since association circumstances and needs will inevitably change over time, dictating new chief executive priorities. Some chief executives are unwilling or unable to accomplish the growth required to tackle new chief executive priorities. In these instances, a parting of the ways does make sense, but it should occur only after the chief executive has been given ample opportunity to consider whether, for him or her, such growth is desirable and feasible.

The classic case is an organization's transition from a period of tremendous growth, fueled by an entrepreneurial chief executive, to one of stability and consolidation. Very few chief executives who excel at leading associations in their entrepreneurial phase are likely to bring the same passion and capability to the more control-oriented phase.

Rules for Interaction

Having agreed on how the chief executive's performance will be judged and the nature and extent of the board's commitment to support his or her performance, the parties can turn to the process side of their relationship, moving away from ends and toward the means to be employed to make the partnership work. The first step in this regard is for the board and chief executive to reach agreement on the overriding values, or principles, that should govern their working relationship, for example:

- openness and honesty in communication and no hidden agendas
- the board's right to know the bad news as well as the good and not to be caught off-guard
- the chief executive's need to have wide latitude in determining the means to be employed to achieve the ends that have been agreed to
- the chief executive's right to accept direction only from the board as a whole and not from individual members
- the chief executive's sole authority to direct staff

In Greater Detail

Then the two parties can move to next level of detail, setting more specific rules to guide their interactions. At the top of any list will be the policies that define the boundaries limiting chief executive activity, such as, for example, the maximum dollar amount that the chief executive can commit without board approval, the chief executive's hiring latitude (anyone as long as budgeted?; only after the board has reviewed a recommended appointment?), and limits on the chief executive's speaking publicly on behalf of the association. Lesser but still important rules might govern the timeliness of the transmittal of written information to the board prior to its being asked to make a decision, the board's communication with staff (for example, direct communication is acceptable, but requests for assistance and direction must come through the chief executive), and the format in which policy recommendations are to be presented.

A Word on Hiring and Directing Staff

As a general rule, if a chief executive officer is to be held accountable for the performance of his or her staff, he or she should have the latitude to recruit and appoint new staff members, to direct their work, and to evaluate their performance. Board involvement in these key executive functions may very well erode chief executive authority and credibility while making the board an accountable party. If the board goes too far, there is no basis for holding the chief executive accountable for his or her subordinates' performance.

It is possible for boards to have some involvement without doing damage. Examples of common practice in this regard include:

- A chief executive shares with the responsible board committee the credentials of the top two or three candidates for a department or program head position, and the committee has an opportunity to meet the chief executive's top choice before affirming the appointment. In this case, two guidelines are advisable. The board should go with the chief executive's first choice unless there are compelling reasons to select one of the other candidates. Any deliberations should be completely confidential, lest a rift between the board and chief executive be perceived.

- Although board members should not participate directly in the evaluation of staff other than the chief executive, board members are often asked to contribute their private assessments of staff dealing closely with them to the chief executive, and chief executives often review their evaluations of top staff before they are communicated to the staff.

Evaluation of Chief Executive Performance

It stands to reason that seriously evaluating the chief executive officer is one of an association board's most important responsibilities. Yet many, if not most, association boards pay relatively little attention to evaluation—until a serious conflict develops. Then, it is often too late to avert a rupture in the partnership and a parting of ways. Many boards do not even attempt to conduct a formal evaluation. Some leave it to the board chair to do; some encourage the chief executive to conduct a self-evaluation, which they merely review. And many continue to use a checklist approach to evaluation, judging chief executive performance along functional (not results) lines, such as team building, management of financial resources, and long-range planning.

Why is chief executive evaluation frequently not done at all, or done in a perfunctory fashion? One deterrent to serious chief executive evaluation appears to be the very natural reluctance of board members to judge a person who is, in practice if not theoretically, the board's peer, especially in light of the adversarial tradition in board-executive relations. Many board members also feel at a distinct disadvantage, knowing far less about the inner workings of their association than the chief executive. And there is just plain lack of knowledge about how to do the job right.

Guidelines for Evaluation

Following a few simple guidelines, an association board can turn the chief executive evaluation process into a powerful tool for improving performance and strengthening the board-chief executive partnership. And in the process, a board can prevent the kind of dramatic clash that often results in a chief executive's abrupt departure, with the attendant negative publicity and dampened internal morale:

Focus on Ends, Not Means

Unless a chief executive violates one of the policies that govern the partnership, such as committing association dollars above the established limit, serious chief executive evaluation should focus on the achievement of specific performance targets at two levels: (1) the association's performance against operational targets set during the planning and budget preparation process, and (2) the individual chief executive performance targets that were negotiated with the board. By focusing on outcomes, the board will come closer to assessing the true effectiveness of chief executive leadership than it could by examining how targets were pursued, which often relates to style more than impact. Of course, when means are pertinent, they should be explicitly factored into the negotiation of performance targets (see Chapter 9 for cases when exceptions to the ends-focus are acceptable).

Focus on Growth, Not Punishment

In evaluating its chief executive's performance, an association board should be more interested in strengthening chief executive performance and growing his or her leadership capability, than merely in determining rewards and punishments. Done in a collegial fashion, evaluation can result in a game plan that a chief executive might follow to improve areas where performance has been weak and in the scaling back of chief executive performance targets that have proved to be unrealistic. This approach is obviously cost effective when one considers the tremendous investment already made in the current chief executive, including the cost of recruitment. Of course, serious repeated performance deficiencies may lead to chief executive termination, but this should happen only after ample warning and serious attempts to work together in remedying them.

Assign Clear Board Accountability

Important governance work tends not to get done in a full and timely fashion if no one on a board is held specifically accountable for doing it—chief executive evaluation is no exception. By assigning responsibility for chief executive evaluation to a standing committee, the board will have taken a big step toward actually getting it done.

Develop a Formal Process and Schedule

The accountable committee should fashion a workplan and timetable to be followed in the process, beginning with the negotiation of performance targets and ending with a formal, written report that conveys both the assessments of performance and the plan for remedying any serious performance shortfalls.

Set Aside Enough Time

Serious, ends-focused evaluation is a complex and time-consuming process that inevitably involves considerable discussion. In addition to an intensive session at which targets are negotiated, one or two three to four-hour work sessions are likely to be needed to accomplish an in-depth assessment of performance and the development of a plan to remedy deficiencies.

Chief Executive Preparation for Partnership

Unfortunately for association chief executives, professional education and training programs have for the most part neglected the subject of board-executive partnerships, and until relatively recently the written sources have been sparse. But experience has taught that chief executives who seriously want to build enduring positive partnerships with their governing boards can take practical affirmative steps to prepare themselves to be effective partners.

Make a Genuine Commitment to a Strong Board

Breaking away from traditional behavior patterns can seem quite risky to an association chief executive, after years of being taught from his or her earliest days in the profession that the only "good" association board is one that keeps at a distance and interferes least. To chief executives taught that their primary role vis a vis the board is to be ever vigilant in guarding against the specter of the board's dabbling in administrative affairs, learning to welcome and to foster the development of a strong board can be a significant challenge.

See the Chief Executive Role as Less Boss and More Architect and Facilitator

The macho notion of the chief executive as the boss at the pinnacle of a command structure, courageously making the tough decisions that come his or her way and refusing to pass on the bucks that reach his or her desk is worse than valueless in today's world; it can actually impede the development of creative partnerships with both the board and the staff. Far more productive is the contemporary notion of the chief executive as both an architect and designer, creatively putting the various pieces of the organization together, and a facilitator, whose key contribution is helping the pieces to function as they are intended. Approaching the board from the perspective of a designer and a facilitator will help an association executive bring greater creativity and flexibility to the partnership building task.

See the Chief Executive as the Board's Peer and Colleague

Regardless of the public myth of a chief executive as basically the top staff person under the board, chief executives who take the more contemporary view of themselves as their boards' peer are more likely to be able to build a strong working partnership. As peers, they will be more likely to take the initiative in relationship building and to be more assertive in their dialogues with their board.

Treat the Board as One of the Association's Most Important and Precious Resources

As I hope this book has made amply clear, an association's board produces powerful outcomes that are critical to association vitality and growth in the areas of planning, operations, and external relations. But the board is a complex, indeed, even delicate, mechanism that must be fine-tuned and well maintained if it is to operate without stalling or malfunctioning. Although a board must take ultimate accountability for its own performance and for the development of its governance capability, its chief executive is the board's top mechanic. He or she pay constant attention to the board's "production process," noting problems and helping the board to resolve them. Chief executives that are successful in playing this role, and in building top-notch partnerships with their boards, tend to devote no less than 25 percent of their time on the average to supporting their boards. And this is quality time, not Sunday-night-at-the-eleventh-hour time.

Know the Board Inside-Out

Boards are people with diverse visions, perspectives, experiences, motivations, attitudes, and capabilities. The deeper the understanding of every board member that the chief executive brings to his or her work with the board, the more successful the partnership is likely to be. For example, knowing that one of her board members has recently taken it on the chin at work and is suffering from low self-esteem as a consequence, an alert and sensitive chief executive can look for an occasion to showcase the depressed board member or to enable him to share the credit for a notable association success. This may sound a trifle hokey and "touchy-feely," but constant care and feeding of this variety is one of the most powerful ways to build a strong relationship, although by no means a substitute for structure and process.

Build a Close Alliance with the Board Chair

The board-chief executive partnership is apt to be much closer if the board chair and chief executive function as a cohesive leadership team. They need to spend considerable time together working out a creative division of labor in the external relations arena and brainstorming ways to strengthen board leadership. The chief executive can help the board chair to carry out his or her leadership role and can ensure that the chair is positioned prominently on ceremonial occasions. No matter how close and friendly the relationship, however, a savvy chief executive will avoid "cutting deals" with a board chair that put the chief executive in the position of taking direction from the chair. A chief executive who is naive enough to get caught in the position of taking direction from both a chair and a board estranged from the chair in some way is in danger of becoming the proverbial sacrificial lamb. Regardless of intent, naiveté seldom arouses sympathy or results in forgiveness.

The Executive Team Role

Association chief executives often designate the staff who head major association operating units and programs as members of an operational coordination group, usually called the executive or management team. Chaired by the chief executive, such teams can play an important role in supporting an association board's performance, for example by:

- coordinating the staff teams that are assigned to work with the board's standing committees, ensuring that they are carrying out their responsibilities fully
- assisting in the development of standing committee and full board agendas
- reviewing material prepared for standing committee and board meetings, such as quarterly financial reports
- critiquing presentations being prepared for special board-staff work sessions, and helping each other upgrade content, format, and presentation styles

An association's executive team can also make a powerful contribution to governing board performance by ensuring that internal planning and management systems that directly support governance are well designed and function effectively, most notably:

- an annual strategic and operational planning and budgeting cycle that builds in significant opportunities for proactive board leadership (see Chapter 9)

- a performance management system that provides pertinent, reliable, and timely information on programmatic and fiscal performance (see Chapter 10)

A Closing Look at Board-Staff Interaction

This chapter has noted that a board can erode its chief executive's authority by giving direction to staff, and that staff should never be allowed to go around the chief executive in lobbying for decisions. However, close board-executive team interaction can enrich the governance process by strengthening the board's understanding of an association's operations and by making executive team members more sensitive to the board's needs and concerns. Significant opportunities for productive, "safe" interaction include standing committee meetings, meetings of standing committee chairs with their staff support team leaders, and, of course, annual strategic and operational planning work sessions.

Chief executives need not worry about staff providing information to board members as requested, just as long as chief executives are kept apprised of such requests and of the information furnished.

Section III

Doing Governance Work

Chapter Nine
Planning as a Board Leadership Tool

Falling Short of Its Potential

Planning surely has no peer as a vehicle for a board's exercise of creative, foresightful leadership. Through the planning process, an association can:

- fashion and keep updated its *strategic framework*—its values, vision, mission, and its broad goals
- identify strategic issues and fashion action strategies to address them
- establish annual performance targets and develop detailed workplans and budgets

Despite its promise, planning has tended in practice in the nonprofit sector to fall far short of its potential, in the process leaving considerable frustration and even cynicism in its wake. All too many association boards have found themselves thumbing through finished tomes that eventually find their way to the proverbial shelf, where they gather dust, rarely consulted by the associations that created them. These same boards are likely year after year to pore over page after number-filled page in the already-finished, line-item budget, asking patently trivial questions.

The problem with this common approach to involving association boards in planning is that if a plan—whether strategic or operational—is finished by the time it reaches a board, there really is nothing important that a board can do with it without impugning the credibility of the chief executive or causing considerable disruption. So boards of well-meaning volunteers are forced to lower their governance sights, either keeping quiet or focusing on relatively mundane matters (as in, "Do we really need to send all staff to the training workshop in Baltimore?"). The reader would not have to look far to find a board spending more time discussing the details of an upcoming conference than it takes to pass a multi-million dollar budget. What an irony!

High Cost of Underachievement

Naturally, in the face of this glaring gap between theory and practice, the average association board member's initial excitement over planning, soon turns to boredom, or worse, to cynicism. After all, she finds herself playing a minor league role in what the world has long called a truly major league leadership process. Ultimately, the cost of board underinvolvement in association planning can be quite high:

- The board as a human resource—a collection of wisdom, experience, perspectives, talents, skills—is sorely underutilized, cheating the association of needed guidance and input.
- The board's enthusiasm for governance and its commitment to the association are eroded.
- The tie that binds the board and its chief executive officer inevitably frays.

Realizing the Promise

No matter how dreary the history of nonprofit planning in practice, association boards and chief executive officers have a tremendous opportunity now to fashion a new alliance—a real team—dedicated to creative collaboration in the planning process. Working closely together, they can ensure that their associations receive a full return on their investment of time, energy, and money in planning—in terms of clearer directions; growth in membership, programs, and revenues; and more effective cost control. They can also ensure that their board is fully engaged in, and energized by, planning.

The good news is that significantly strengthening an association's planning process and incorporating a strong, creative board role into planning do not have to cost an arm and a leg. We are not talking about fancy high-tech process, with humming computers and exotic analytical techniques. Nor does advancement on the planning front mean that we have to embrace some planning fad, such as the current inflation of total quality management from a useful set of operating techniques to the system that will turn us around. Rather, like most truly important things that happen in nonprofit leadership, we are talking about the well-designed and carefully orchestrated involvement of human beings in using information to deliberate and make decisions in an orderly fashion.

Five Key Factors

Five key factors loom largest in making sure an association board's involvement in planning yields powerful results:

- **Planning Cycle**—Fashioning a comprehensive planning process or cycle for the association that clearly identifies what the outcomes will be, the schedule of activities involved in producing them, and the roles that the board, chief executive, and staff are to play in the process

- **Clear Board Role**—Spelling out a role for the board at key points in the process where proactive leadership—not just reaction—is practically (not theoretically) possible

- **Time Commitment**—Board members' committing the required time to play this enhanced leadership role in planning (the time to participate in creating a vision statement for an association will greatly exceed the time needed merely to review a staff draft of the vision.)

- **Executive Support**—Strong chief executive and staff support for the board's enhanced role, including, when feasible, appointment of a full-time staff planning officer to coordinate the planning activities

- **Board Planning Committee**—A board planning committee that focuses on working closely with the chief executive and staff in designing and implementing the planning process

Chief Executive Leadership

Strategic and operational planning are usually described as among the most important of all executive functions, and chief executives typically have been taught to keep a tight hold on the planning reins, providing boards with well-crafted documents that leave little room for adjustment. Boards can play a significant, creative role in planning only if chief executives are open to going beyond these traditional constraints, sharing the planning action with their boards and relaxing control.

Through such creative sharing, a chief executive can ensure that his or her board actually does more important work and consequently feels greater satisfaction. The board-chief executive working relationship will improve without fail, and, contrary to the conventional wisdom, the board will become less involved in minute details. Boards that dabble in minor matters usually do so in lieu of more important things to do.

Goodbye, Tractor Plans

The field of nonprofit strategy is in rapid transition. Traditional strategic long-range planning (known variously as comprehensive master planning, five-year planning, or just plain old strategic planning) is rapidly giving way to new approaches—for very sound reasons. Old-time, long-range planning, with its thousands of words and pounds of paper, was based on the assumption that the world around an organization would change in predictable ways and, hence, that an organization's current programs and activities could be projected in detail into the future. Even the preferred time horizons—3, 5, or even 10 years are totally arbitrary and have no relationship to any natural rhythm in human affairs.

Many Words But Little Action

So nonprofit organizations, including a number of associations, fashioned monster long-range plans, typically consisting of a set of five-year goals as an umbrella for detailed, year-by-year projections of program activities. Faced with the prospect of having to project what they were doing into an unknown future, staff very sensibly used mechanistic approaches to moving their programs forward (as in 5 percent increases per year for five years). Of course, the preeminent example of such mechanistic planning was the former Soviet state's elaborate agricultural and industrial plans, religiously updated every year and stunningly irrelevant in practice. It is likely that never in human history have so many well-intentioned words produced so little positive impact and so many forests been point-lessly sacrificed.

Topsy-Turvy World

The fact is, such control-oriented planning never worked because the world does not oblige our associations by changing in predictable ways. This is a topsy-turvy world, as Tecker and Fidler point out in *Successful Association Leadership*:

> We now find ourselves in a period of time when change is much more rapid and much less continuous . . . . A larger portion of the most significant changes impacting associations are caused by events that are increasingly less predictable. The certainly of past predictable trend curves no longer exists. The graphic depiction of change today looks more like an electrocardiogram. It comprises high peaks and low valleys occurring in more compressed time spans than ever experienced before.

Why It Still Exists

If traditional long-range planning so obviously fails to fit the world we live and work in and produces such puny impact for the immense effort it takes, why do we still find examples of its being practiced, even today? Beyond the siren song of tradition and normal human inertia, the continued life of such a patently ineffective process is probably accounted for by:

- **Illusion of Control**—The comfort that comes from the feeling of being in control and hence secure in a bewildering, threatening world, even though the control is illusory. It is the list that mildly compulsive achievers make every morning—writ large. In reality, such comfort, based on an illusion, can actually make an association much more vulnerable than if it had done no long-range planning at all.
- **Retro Chief Executives**—The occasional chief executive officer, who, consciously or not, is basically defensive in dealing with his or her board, and prefers board members to be so busy plowing through massive tomes that they do not have the time to dabble in his or her affairs.

Emergence of Strategic Management

Fortunately for associations committed to doing serious strategic planning and involving their boards powerfully in the process, over the past quarter-century a tremendously important variation on the strategic planning theme—usually known as strategic management—has developed as an antidote to the deficiencies of conventional long range planning. Strategic management is recognizable by its:

- elevation of association vision to the driver's seat in the planning process, the guide and goad that determines an association's future course

- attention to the external environment, realistically, in detail, and free of wishful thinking

- equal attention to internal resources and strengths and weaknesses, as the foundation on which strategy must rest

- selectivity, in that it focuses on specific change initiatives to address specific strategic issues, rather than merely projecting present activities into the future

- action-bias, concentrating on actually implementing change now to deal with issues the association sees now

- attention to change management—thinking through in detail strategies for overcoming resistance and facilitating the implementation of change initiatives

- freedom from arbitrary time frames—recognizing that strategies to address selected strategic issues will have unique time requirements and that it makes no sense to plan for meaningless and arbitrary chunks of time that have nothing to do with implementation schedules

- letting operational planning and budget do its job—not attempting to project forward beyond a year the detailed operational plans and budgets of an association, but letting the budget process handle the essential job of refining and incrementally changing operational plans annually

- eschewing grandiosity—assuming that implementable changes must come in "chewable bites" that can actually be managed, rather than just talked about. The resources in money, staff, and time of virtually all associations are precious and highly constrained, and most change initiatives that are launched cannot draw on a $1 million-plus innovation fund of some kind. Instead, associations must work hard to find modest chunks of time and money to invest in change.

Two Fundamental Agendas

Successfully applying strategic management techniques requires making a distinction between two broad streams of association activity—two huge agendas—that must be kept apart and managed separately. If the two are mixed up, creative, significant change is highly unlikely to survive the press of day-to-day events (see Figure 6).

STRATEGIC: Innovation, Change, Growth

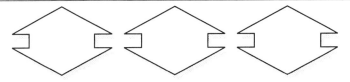

OPERATIONAL: Running The Shop

Figure 6. Two Fundamental Agendas

The Operational Agenda—Running the Shop

Running the shop is the bread and butter agenda of every association, providing the most visible and immediate benefits to the membership. We typically use the annual operational plan and budget to organize this agenda. Such practices as Monday morning executive team meetings and monthly financial reports are reliable operational management tools.

The Strategic Agenda—Innovating, Changing, Growing

This agenda has to do with selecting association change and development targets— above and beyond current operational activities—and implementing strategies intended to achieve the targets.

VISION:
Where / What We Want To Be

Change Initiatives

- Seizing Opportunities
- Overcoming Barriers

CURRENT SITUATION:
Revenues / Programs / Services / Customers

Figure 7. Strategic Management in a Nutshell

Fashioning the Strategic Change Portfolio

In a nutshell, strategic management is a very practical and cost-effective device for determining how an association should innovate and change in major ways, while continuing to operate its budgeted programs and manage its day-to-day affairs. The strategic management process can be scheduled and integrated into a formal planning cycle and timetable, as we shall see below, but truly strategic associations and individuals tend to practice strategic management techniques continuously.

Narrowing the Strategic Gap

The strategic management process is basically intended to narrow the gap between an association's vision of what it wants to be and do and where it is now—its current mission, programs, and activities (see Figure 7). Without a clear, detailed vision, of course, an association cannot determine where it needs to change to narrow the gap, and hence serious visioning is an indispensable first step in the process. Within the "strategic gap," an association, if it looks hard enough, will identify strategic issues. These are major barriers in the way—and important opportunities to advance toward—the association's vision. In fashioning change initiatives to address the issues that are selected for attention now, the association will create its own strategic change portfolio. This change portfolio cannot merely be lumped into an association's ongoing day-to-day management, which would overwhelm it, but, instead, must be consciously managed as an entirely separate association agenda (See Chapter 13 for more detail on managing change).

Key Steps

An association going through its own strategic management process in the quest of its own strategic change portfolio will take the following steps (many of which can be accomplished in a retreat setting involving the association board) (Figure 8):

- **Updating the Association Strategic Framework**—its values, vision, and mission
- **Scanning the External and Internal Environments**—getting a handle on external conditions and trends, assessing internal resources, and identifying strengths and weaknesses
- **Identifying Strategic Issues**—the barriers and opportunities that appear to be of associationwide significance
- **Selecting Issues Deserving Immediate Attention**
- **Fashioning Strategic Initiatives to Address the Issues**
- **Managing Implementation of the Initiatives**

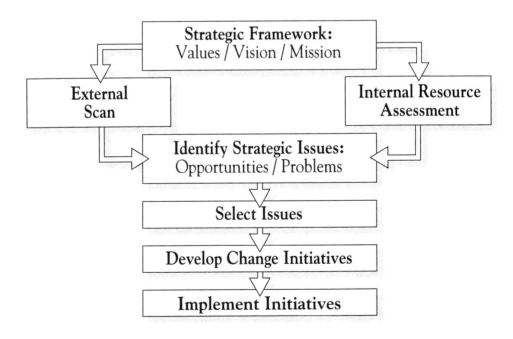

Figure 8. Strategic Management Flow

Board Involvement

Boards can play a creative, in-depth, and influential role at certain points in the strategic management process, which both fit the board's high-level governance mission and provide significant leverage: developing and confirming an association's values, vision, and mission; identifying and selecting the strategic issues that demand attention; reviewing and approving strategic change initiatives; and monitoring implementation of the initiatives.

An excellent device for kicking-off a strategic management process with in-depth board participation is a one or one-and-a-half-day board-chief executive-staff retreat in which participants explore the association vision and mission, assess the internal and external environments, identify strategic issues, and brainstorm possible initiatives. Of course, a retreat (discussed in detail in Chapter 12) cannot do the whole job in one fell swoop; considerable activity must follow, including selection of the initiatives, detailed action planning, and monitoring.

Association Vision—Beyond Mere Dreaming

Vision is without doubt both the intelligence and the driver of strategy. Without a clear, detailed vision as a starting point, an association's strategic management process will be far less capable of identifying the most important strategic issues to be addressed. For both associations and the individuals who comprise them, strategy without vision can easily become motion without direction, and experience has taught us all that being busy does not necessarily mean being productive.

In the nonprofit sector, unfortunately, vision has remained a somewhat vague concept with little obvious utility in developing organizational strategies. Its tremendous potential for organizational good is, therefore, seldom realized in practice. Popularly and somewhat vaguely seen as having to do with fundamental purposes, inspiration, and motivation, vision is often erroneously seen as a kind of pie-in-the-sky dreaming or used interchangeably with its close—but very different—ally, mission.

Vision is basically a picture of the long-range future, and the more detailed the vision, the more useful it can be in identifying and selecting strategic issues. In doing visioning, it is important, by the way, that associations distinguish between serious planning, on the one hand, and public relations and information activities, on the other. While a pithy paragraph that attractively captures the essence of an association's vision will very likely make sense for association public relations purposes, a far more detailed and unvarnished version is much more useful in the internal, strategic-management process.

An association's long-range future can be envisioned in three basic ways:

1. A values vision describes an association's most cherished beliefs and principles, relative both to its work in the wider environment and to its internal culture.

2. An impact vision describes the most fundamental impacts that an association's efforts are intended to have on its environment over the long-run.

3. An image vision describes how an association wants to be perceived by its own members, key constituents, and the wider public.

The associations cited in the remainder of this chapter exist, and the examples presented are drawn from their real-life experiences in applying strategic management techniques.

Values Vision

The Women's City Club of Cleveland determined that the club's preeminent values naturally divided into four broad categories: club members' responsibilities; club members' personal development; community service; and internal culture. Examples from the lengthy list that was developed in a one-and-a-half-day board retreat include: "the worth of women;" "cultural diversity;" "education and knowledge as gifts to be shared;" "life-long learning;" "civic involvement;" "high ethical standards;" "professionalism;" "high quality and excellence in services;" "recognition of accomplishment;" "creative change;" "teamwork;" "help for others less fortunate."

The Savannah Area Chamber of Commerce (in Georgia) identified as core values "an economic climate that fosters growth;" "business-education collaboration in building high-quality public education;" "stronger community leadership capability;" "accountability;" and "creativity and innovation."

The board, executive team, and invited planning participants of the Anxiety Disorders Association of America (Rockville, Maryland) named among the association's most important values: "the seriousness of anxiety disorders as an illness and the importance of providing help to people suffering from anxiety disorders;" "easy access to information about anxiety disorders and to treatment;" and "outreach that transcends economic, social, cultural, racial, and ethnic boundaries."

Impact Vision

An association's impact vision identifies the most fundamental positive changes that it envisions its efforts will produce in its environment. The board and chief executive officer of the Health Industry Distributors Association (HIDA) (Alexandria, Virginia) fashioned an impact vision including: "more profitable and productive and better informed members;" "more business and dollars flowing through distributors;" "a greater distributor impact on national policy formulation and issue resolution;" "more competitive members in the managed care arena;" "enhanced efficiency in the supply channel;" "stronger member involvement in HIDA affairs."

The National Council of Jewish Women—Cleveland Section envisioned as major impacts: "community and political leaders will better understand and more strongly protect such core rights as privacy and church-state separation;" "the non-Jewish community will better understand and support the Jewish community;" "the nonprofit service sector in Greater Cleveland will be characterized by more active cooperation and collaboration;" "a strong framework for the involvement of future generations of volunteers will be created."

The Anxiety Disorders Association of America envisioned that among its major long-term impacts would be: "wider understanding of anxiety disorders and recognition of its seriousness;" "universal access to effective and affordable treatment;" "public policy vis a vis anxiety disorder that promotes full parity in medical insurance coverage and nondiscrimination in employment;" "increase in prevention and early intervention;" "significant growth in the number of minority professionals in the anxiety disorders field;" "significant reduction in misdiagnosis and mistreatment of anxiety disorders;" "wide availability of detailed treatment guidelines based on demonstrated efficacy."

The Ohio Job Training Partnership, Inc., envisioned that its principal long-term impacts would include: "a stronger economy in Ohio;" "more individual self-sufficiency;" "wider understanding of the value and content of employment and training in Ohio;" "stronger communication, cooperation, and collaborative planning and program development among human service agencies;" and "more influential and effective Private Industry Councils."

And the Agency-Company Organization for Research and Development (Pearl River, New York) envisioned as results of its efforts:

"improvement in the success and survival rates of agencies and companies;" "better agency and company understanding and utilization of technology;" "reduction in the cost of doing business in the property/casualty industry;" "the independent agency system's gaining a dramatically larger market share;" "a more efficient delivery system as a result of the different parts working together more effectively;" and "increasing cooperation in the industry."

Image Vision

Although fashioning a clear image is intended to support and facilitate achievement of an association vision and mission, image takes its place as a co-equal with the other key components of vision because of its power. Like it or not, effective programs, high-quality services, and capable management do not always speak for themselves and often go unrecognized and uncredited. And a single misstep, if widely publicized, can stick firmly in the public's mind, providing a negative lens through which to see the unfortunate association's operations, regardless of its actual performance. So while a strong positive image cannot make up for an association's poor performance over an extended period, it can facilitate public recognition of excellence and can help an association to survive visible mishaps. The image vision also provides a clear, detailed framework within which external relations strategies can be fashioned.

The envisioned image of the Women's City Club of Cleveland includes such characteristics as: "influential;" "independent;" "nonpolitical;" "innovative and cutting edge;" "warm and welcoming;" "THE club to join—'movers and shakers' in the community;" "creative in deploying resources;" "focused and purposeful;" "a stimulating place to be."

The Savannah Area Chamber of Commerce wants to be seen as: "an essential resource for business start-up and development;" "progressive and cutting-edge;" "cooperative and collaborative;" "organized and efficient;" "user friendly;" "a catalyst for community planning and long-term economic growth;" "a strong advocate for small business;" "committed to addressing civic development issues;" "a 'heavy hitter'; in the community;" "noncompetitive;" "open and receptive;" and "dedicated to the growing involvement and leadership development of minorities and women."

And the Anxiety Disorders Association of America envisions that it will be seen as: "the nation's preeminent organization for anxiety disorders sufferers, their families and friends, and for those involved in treating anxiety disorders;" "a major direction-setter and supporter for powerful research in the field;" "a top-quality organization that can be counted on for its reliability and effectiveness;" "an influential organization with such clout that policy makers take heed;" "an inclusive, welcoming organization;" and "a good partner (easy to work with)."

The Vision-Mission Connection

The reader must wonder how an association's vision differs from its mission and how they work together in the strategic management process. In a nutshell, if vision is a multifaceted picture of an association's long-term future, its mission is a detailed picture of that association now, in terms of its members and customers, its products and services, and the roles it plays and technologies it employs in producing and delivering its products and services. As is true with vision, an association can always use the several components of a detailed mission to craft a succinct, appealing statement for public consumption. This abbreviated public version is a public relations product and should not be confused with the detailed mission that is essential for serious strategic management.

Vision and mission are not only different in content, they also serve completely different purposes. Vision is intended to inspire and to motivate an association and to guide it in selecting strategic issues to tackle. Mission is more a disciplinary tool, establishing clear boundaries and fighting the "headless chicken" syndrome. Vision moves an association in new directions. Mission keeps it from losing its head in willy-nilly expansion and diversification.

Over time, if an association seriously applies strategic management as a planning tool, vision will expand and pressure mission to change. Strategic issues in the form of barriers and opportunities will inevitably be identified to close the gap between long-range aspirations (an association's vision) and what the association is right now (its mission). Vision will force fundamental directional questions to be raised and dramatic new possibilities to be considered, while mission will force second thoughts and resist undue haste. Without a clear, detailed mission, an association will be in much greater danger of falling victim to the "everything to everybody" syndrome. However, a clear mission that is not pressured by a strong, expansive vision can lead to a hardening of an association's arteries and even to its eventual obsolescence.

For example, the Health Industry Distributors Association, in fashioning its detailed mission statement in an intensive day-long work session, identified as its key customers its member distributors directly and, less directly, nonmember distributors, manufacturers, and suppliers. It then identified the major products and services provided to each customer group. For example, the distributor members of HIDA receive: education and training, information, research, lobbying, an annual trade show, an executive conference, a set of publications, and technical assistance in management information and electronic data interface. And finally, so that their mission would be far more serious than the typical shopping list of aspirations, the HIDA board and chief executive determined how they were delivering these key products and the relative priority of each product, as measured by the resources allocated to its production.

Strategic Issues—An Overview

In addition to fashioning association vision and mission statements, boards, their chief executives and staff can also identify critical strategic issues facing the association (usually in a retreat setting) and even begin, if not finish, the job of choosing the issues that will be tackled during the current planning cycle. Strategic issues, which come in diverse shapes and sizes, are basically "change challenges" in the form of opportunities to move toward an association's vision and of barriers or problems that are likely to impede progress toward realizing the vision.

Strategic issues can relate to a wide range of association activity, for example:

- **Members, Customers, Programs, Revenues**—the opportunity to address changing member needs and to provide new services to a new customer; the decline of a traditional revenue source that forces an association to search for new revenues

- **Image and External Relations**—the need to build an image that more closely fits the evolving vision of the association as a means to strengthen membership; a frayed relationship with a key stakeholder whose support is essential for the implementation of an important new program
- **Organizational Leadership, Planning, and Management Capability**—the need to upgrade a management system (say, financial management) whose deficiencies threaten to seriously weaken association performance and to consume an inordinate amount of executive time; an internal morale problem that is eroding the quality of member services; weaknesses in governance that are causing large-scale frustration and some anger among board members

When Are Issues Strategic?

How can a board and the executive team decide when an issue is really strategic, thus demanding special attention at a high level, or just an operational issue that can be handled through the normal operational planning and management process? While identifying strategic issues involves more subjective judgment than scientific logic, certain characteristics tell us that an issue is likely to be strategic:

1. **High Stakes**—A strategic issue demands attention because the likely cost of not dealing with it in the near future is expected to be high, in terms of lost benefits or direct penalties, or both. Failure to tackle a promising new funding opportunity may result in a fiscal crisis down the road, and not responding in a timely fashion to changing member needs may lead to serious membership decline.

2. **Intensive Attention**—An issue can be so complex, and the need for action in the near-term so pressing, that the issue cannot be left to an association's routine planning and management process or merely be delegated to a staff person.

3. **Cross-Cutting**—Very often, strategic issues just do not fit into any existing association operating unit or program and can very easily fall through the proverbial cracks. A program being developed in response to changing member needs may have no organizational home and not fall into the bailiwick of any member of the executive team. Such above-the-line matters as board capability building by definition fall in this category.

For example, the Health Industry Distributors Association's list of strategic issues, identified over the course of a one-and-a-half-day board-chief executive retreat, included: the need to rethink the division of its member volunteers into certain market segments in light of rapid restructuring of the health care field; the need to fashion a clear strategy for HIDA's home health care business; the need to upgrade significantly public understanding of HIDA; and the opportunity to make the annual trade show a more successful event, financially and programmatically.

The Savannah Area Chamber of Commerce concluded over the course of a two-day strategic work session that a cumbersome governance process and structure was a major barrier to future growth. Other pressing issues were the Chamber's image in the community and the participation of small businesses in chamber affairs.

And the Anxiety Disorders Association of America board and executive team identified among the more pressing issues facing the association the need to develop a stronger membership program and to think through the association's place in the rapidly evolving health care system.

Selecting Issues

Selecting the strategic issues to be addressed during the current planning cycle is another step that lends itself to intensive board-staff deliberation. This can occur either as part of a retreat where the issues have been identified, or in a follow-up work session, for which additional staff analysis has been conducted to facilitate the selection process. Selection is an indispensable step since the overriding objective to the strategic management process is *action*—and change—in the near-term. Old-time supermarket style planning, with its shopping lists of tantalizing possibilities, does not work in this regard. The cruel fact is that no association, no matter how large in membership, staff, and budget, can handle every strategic issue it identifies at one time, while continuing to handle its day-to-day activities well. *Selectivity is the name of the strategic management game, and an association that is serious about the process will treat selection as a high priority step.*

Change on the Margin

It is important to keep in mind while going through the selection process that most associations differ greatly from General Motors, forcing them to be quite modest in launching change initiatives to address strategic issues. The challenge for the average association is to find some time, and perhaps a little money, to deal with two, three, or four serious issues at any given time, while continuing to spend 98 percent of resources on keeping the shop running (see Figure 9). It stands to reason, then, that the average association must choose issues that it can realistically handle. Far from being earth-shaking or grandiose, to be manageable the strategic issues must be in "chewable bites" that will not overwhelm the association.

Figure 9. Change on the Margin

Narrowing the List

Narrowing down a list of 50 tantalizing candidates for strategic issue status to four "chewable bites" that an association can afford to address is more an art than a science. However, the board in collaboration with the chief executive and staff can bring rigorous logic and common sense to the selection task by asking certain key questions:

1. What is our association likely to pay as penalties if we do not deal with a particular issue this year? Penalties typically take the form of direct damage (an eroding relationship, an alienated stakeholder, a budget cut) or less direct consequences (such as missing a major new grant opportunity or not securing a new market).

2. Is our association realistically capable of tackling a particular issue, either alone or in alliance with one or more stakeholders? We may need to build stronger staff capability or raise new revenues to address a particular issue. What are the odds that we can muster the resources that will enable us to address the issue?

3. What risks are involved in tackling a particular issue? Is it politically or technically complex enough to make risk a serious issue? Is it so controversial that by merely tackling it we might lose significant support among our membership?

The board, chief executive, and executive team may decide that there is no choice but to address certain issues because the penalties for failing to act are so severe. Usually, however, such easy and dramatic decisions do not come an association's way very often. More often, the board, chief executive, and executive team must do a balancing act, choosing a small number of issues that promise the greatest association benefits—those that are assessed as affordable and manageable, and that involve the most favorable ratio of benefits to costs.

Next Steps

At this point in the strategic management process, after the strategic issues have been selected, most association boards will probably want to move to a more aloof, oversight posture as the process of fashioning change initiatives (usually by in-house task forces)and committing resources to their implementation (always by formal board adoption of strategy) moves forward. However, whether association board members participate in some way in fashioning change initiatives, or just review recommendations from task forces later in the process, is a matter of board-chief executive design. As usual, there is no one "right" answer. However an association board chooses to proceed from this point on, it should ensure, together with the chief executive, that the process is carefully designed. In this regard, the following guidelines will be helpful.

Employing Task Forces

Once the issues that need to be immediately tackled, have been selected, it makes good sense to put together task forces to accomplish the detailed action strategy formulation that comes next. Task forces are most effective as a planning tool when:

- **They Draw Staff from Different Program and Functional Areas in an Association—** Since strategic issues significantly impact the whole association and since they tend to cut across functions and organizational divisions, task forces with diverse membership are essential. An added benefit of task forces is that they enhance internal communication and build a stronger internal culture.
- **They Involve Key Stakeholders**—Stakeholders can bring critical experience, expertise, and knowledge to the strategy formulation process. Their involvement can be a means to strengthen ties, as well as build stakeholder commitment to implementation of task-force recommendations.
- **They Are Well Led**—Choosing the right task-force leaders will help to ensure that their work is accomplished in a full and timely fashion. In making the appointments, look for (1) a strong understanding of, and commitment to, the strategy formulation process; (2) well-developed planning and facilitation skills; (3) the ability to relate well to peers; (4) openness to new ideas; and (5) an inclination to pay meticulous attention to detail.
- **They Receive a Clear, Detailed Charge**—Since strategic issues can be very different, the strategies to address them can also differ significantly, as can the methodologies to produce

the strategies. For example, a task force whose charge is to develop the plan for a possible merger with another association will be producing a very different product than a task force whose charge is to fashion strategy to tap a new revenue source, or to develop new product ideas to address new membership needs. These obvious differences mean that, if task forces are to hit the ground running, and to maintain their momentum, they must receive clear, detailed guidance about the job they are to perform: the precise nature of their strategic product, the methodology they are to employ, and the deadlines they are to meet.

- **The Constraints Are Made Perfectly Clear**—A critical supplement to a task-force charge is the constraints that will govern their work. The board and chief executive might, for example, decide that the only acceptable strategy involving new expenditures will clearly identify a new funding source and will include a detailed plan for tapping it. Or they may decide that certain subjects are clearly off-limits, perhaps because of their political sensitivity. Whatever the constraints, by stating them at the onset, valuable time will be saved and needless emotion avoided.

- **Their Work Is Overseen and Coordinated**—To ensure the task-force process moves forward as planned, it is important that a staff person be assigned to oversee and it and that the board regularly review progress.

- **They Develop a Detailed Task-Force Workplan**—In addition to reviewing their charge at their first organizational meeting, it is important that each task force fashion a detailed workplan to meet the deadlines that have been assigned. The workplan should clearly identify and schedule the tasks to be accomplished, and should assign specific jobs to each task-force member.

Strategy Formulation Methodology

The precise methodology that an association task force employs in carrying out its strategy formulation charge must be tailored to the particular issues being addressed. However, the great majority of task forces will produce one primary product—a set of what we might call "change initiatives" to address the issue assigned to the task force. A change initiative can be thought of as a specific action strategy aimed at accomplishing specific targets and will consist of the:

- statement of the need (or subissues) being addressed
- specific targets to be achieved by the initiative
- action plan to achieve the targets
- required resources

As we shall see in the following section, an association board can review and adopt the change initiatives recommended by its task forces as part of the annual operational planning and budget phase of the association's annual planning cycle.

Cockroach or Clydesdale?

The annual operational plan and budget document is often called the board's preeminent policy statement. While that may overstate the case, there is no question that the very familiar line-item, object-of-expenditure budget does its cost-control job quite effectively, with little muss or fuss. Budgets, unlike strategies, are routinely produced year after year, and they are actually used to manage associations. This cockroach of planning tools is perhaps the hardiest of survivors, going about its business with few admirers, generating little excitement, and being generally impervious to fancy reform efforts (from once popular zero-based budgeting to currently ballyhooed quality management approaches).

By its very nature a conservative and control-oriented process, budget preparation typically involves making incremental adjustments in current program activities and expenditure plans to ensure that an association's revenues and expenditures remain in balance throughout the fiscal year. The process of producing the annual budget usually involves association boards at the tail end, when about all they can do is to sift through an incredible amount of detail, asking relatively minor questions. While formally adopting the budget may, indeed, constitute a major policy statement, association boards traditionally play a minor role in guiding the budget's development.

However, without losing the cost-control benefits that barebones financial budgeting confers on an association, we can transform our modest cockroach into a much more glamorous beast—a kind of Clydesdale of planning tools, capable of bearing a much more impressive policy load. The key is to focus much more board and staff attention on the operational planning that precedes budget preparation and to identify points where the board can exercise serious policy guidance.

Focus on Results, Not Dollars

In designing a more powerful operational planning prelude to putting together an association's financial budget, we must keep in mind that for most associations allocating available dollars to programs, activities, and objects of expenditure is a highly constrained process with little potential for serious policy making. Current programs are generally carried forward into the future, with incremental adjustments to cover inflationary increases, and with program enhancements paid for by minor reallocations within established budget limits. And new programs are most often tied to specific revenue increases or to new sources such as grants. Funding new programs by phasing out ineffective ones is much more common in theory than in practice.

Rising above the dollars, a board, in partnership with the chief executive and staff, can exercise significant influence in the operational planning process by paying attention to the outcomes to be achieved, the performance measures to be employed in measuring their achievement, significant innovations in program operations, and any policy issues related to achieving the outcomes that need to be resolved before the new fiscal year begins.

Intensive Dialogue, Not Just Paper

A tried-and-true means for addressing the outcomes, performance measures, innovations, and implementation policies is to stage a day-long operational planning retreat well in advance of preparation and review of the financial budget, involving the board (or perhaps its planning committee), the chief executive, and the executive team (major operating unit or program heads). The simple step of putting all of the key participants together in the same room for several hours, and providing them with pertinent information in an easily understandable and useful format, will significantly strengthen association operational planning.

A casual, retreat setting, with participants seated in collegial fashion in a horseshoe arrangement will foster dialogue. More important, each major operating unit or program head can facilitate dialogue by making highly focused presentations, preferably employing slides, rather than overwhelming board members with blobs of paper. Such presentations might consist of:

- a program's updated mission statement (products and services, customers and clients, operating functions)
- the program's organizational structure and current budget
- significant environmental changes pertinent to the unit's mission and plans, including changing needs and technologies
- planned outcomes and accomplishments for the coming year beyond routine functions, including significant planned innovations in both administration and service delivery
- any policy-level issues affecting program implementation that appear to merit board attention, including anticipated major new expenditures that will appear in the ultimate recommended expenditure budget if the board agrees
- an implementation plan consisting of key milestones that will serve as performance indicators for board monitoring purposes

The dialogue is likely to be much more fruitful if each member of the executive team spends between 30 and 60 minutes in direct communication with the board, responding to questions and addressing concerns in addition to making the presentation. And a written report, summarizing all of the key points made during the discussion, should be distributed to all participants within a week or so after the session.

A well-planned operational planning retreat along the foregoing lines can produce substantial benefits for the association that conducts it in terms of:

1. **Board Understanding**—The opportunity to engage in an intensive dialogue directly with the major operating unit or program heads, supported by a focused visual presentation, will strengthen the board's understanding—at a high level—of an association's work, the people who are accountable for the accomplishment of that work, and the resources fueling the work. Any board that participates in such a session will be well prepared to review the financial budget that is ultimately recommended for adoption.

2. **Policy Direction**—A financial budget conveys policy assumptions only implicitly, if they can be found at all. By requiring that executive team members give serious thought to, and explicitly describe, any policy issues that drive their operational plans, the board is given an opportunity to provide serious direction in shaping the financial budget.

3. **Board-Staff Relations**—Interaction in a casual, low-pressure setting without the need to take immediate action and with few if any "face" questions involved is a good way to foster mutual board and staff understanding of each other's concerns and perspectives and to promote more effective board-staff teamwork.

4. **Planning Content**—The requirement to prepare a demanding visual presentation for a highly visible and, by definition, a high stakes meeting with an association's board will ensure that executive team members give considerable attention to the planning process and will inevitably upgrade the content of operating plans.

5. **Executive Team Building**—An executive team preparing for a day-long session with its board will be well advised to engage in intensive collective preparation, critiquing each other's presentations as thoroughly as feasible, looking at content, format, and presentation style.

The Strategic Planning and Operational Planning Nexus

Despite the oft-espoused theory that describes operational planning and budget preparation as taking place in the context of the strategic umbrella, which somehow infuses it with direction and meaning, strategic and operational plans and budgets have traditionally gone their own merry ways with no practical ties. Typically, strategic plans were produced, read, admired—perhaps even fondled once or twice—then shelved and never again consulted. Then operational plans and budgets were produced. The twain never met—except theoretically, in planners' heads.

As strategic management has replaced traditional long-range planning, the nexus between strategic and operational plans has been rethought. First, it is accepted that the two serve basically different purposes. Strategic management is intended to identify and address high-stakes issues that are of associationwide significance and that are above the line, not fitting within existing programs and operating units. The operational planning and budget process is a tried-and-true vehicle for refining and reconfiguring existing programs and operations.

Now, having accepted the inherent, and very fundamental differences, between the two planning processes, every association must make two essential connections between the two (Figure 10):

1. Every program and major operating unit should take into account its association's strategic framework in updating its operational plans and budget: explicitly responding to the updated association values, vision, and mission in its operational planning. Nothing prevents board members' asking how unit heads have addressed the evolving strategic framework during the annual operational planning retreat.

2. Strategy formulation task forces created to address strategic issues that are identified and selected in the annual strategic-planning session can report their recommendations at the annual operational session, at which time the costs of implementing the strategies can be addressed.

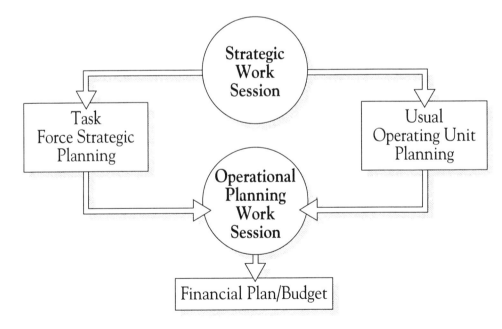

Figure 10. Strategic-Operational Planning Nexus

Chapter Ten
Performance Oversight

Plans Don't Implement Themselves

Visions, missions, and plans are not self-implementing. As the reader well knows, the path from aspirations and intentions to actual performance is often tortuous and blocked by unanticipated hurdles. While association chief executives and their executive teams are responsible for fashioning sound implementation plans and for carrying them out on time and within budget, association boards are ultimately accountable to their members, major stakeholders, and the public-at-large for the translation of intent into action. An association board must, therefore, become involved in assessing its association's progress toward achieving vision and mission and in comparing its actual to planned performance.

The Stakes Are High

This major board responsibility is growing in importance, as a recent *Harvard Business Review* article points out, "in an economy that demands increased organizational efficiency and in a society that demands increased accountability." Indeed, in today's world—with the media caught up in Watergate-spawned exposé journalism and with an increasingly cynical public whose appetite for revelations of wrongdoing seems insatiable—the consequences of major missteps can be costly, if not deadly. Membership and revenues can decline, a stellar reputation can be sullied overnight, political influence can precipitously wane, and future fund-raising efforts can be jeopardized.

In this environment, good stewardship means more than being an aloof board that waits until the close of the fiscal year to reflect on accomplishments and to evaluate financial and programmatic performance. It is not enough these days for an association board to sit back and dole out rewards and punishments after the fact. No board today has any choice but to play an active role in monitoring an association's performance on an ongoing basis, in creative partnership with its chief executive officer.

More Than Digesting Information

Effective board performance oversight is easier to talk about generally than to put into actual practice. Witness the frequency with which nonprofit boards around the country have been caught off guard by revelations of executive mismanagement and by dramatic shortfalls in organizational performance. We know from experience that a board's merely being well informed does not mean it is rigorously monitoring an association's performance. Many board members dutifully digest reams of paper describing their associations' accomplishments and activities and sit through hours of staff briefings.

However, despite their impressive information base, such well-informed boards often are not engaged in serious performance monitoring and cannot say with any assurance how well their associations are actually doing at a given point in time. Indeed, well-briefed, highly knowledgeable boards that are not able to hold their staff accountable are probably the rule rather than the exception in association management.

Effective Oversight

Why have so many knowledgeable, hard-working association boards had so much difficulty carrying out their performance oversight role? There is wide agreement on one reason: The very nature of the nonprofit enterprise militates against performance monitoring. Houle points out that nonprofit boards "have a special difficulty, because, unlike their contemporaries in the business world, they do not have a central measure of success."

But lacking the definitive financial measures (the "bottom line") that for-profit organizations can apply in assessing performance, does not excuse nonprofit associations from their performance oversight responsibility; rather, it makes creative, intensive attention to oversight even more important. In this regard, a committed association board in alliance with its chief executive officer must take three key steps on the road to effective performance oversight:

Set Targets—Developing measurable association performance targets and identifying critical milestones required to achieve the targets is the indispensable first step.

Determine What We Need to Know—Identifying the information required to measure achievement of the targets and determining how and when it can be most effectively reported is the next step.

Decide What We Will Do with It—Determining how the reported information can be analyzed, reviewed, and used in making decisions is the final key step.

The answers to these three questions comprise an association board's performance oversight design, which is heavily influenced by an association's strategic and operational planning process.

An Operations Committee

Several association boards have found that it makes good sense to create a standing operations or management committee with responsibility for board performance oversight. Such a committee can engage the chief executive, chief financial officer, and other association executives in creative dialogue about the design of a performance oversight process that will provide the board with real teeth. In this comfortable, less formal setting than a full board meeting, board and staff members can explore ways to cut through the all-too-common ritual that substitutes for serious monitoring, ensuring that the board is involved in a meaningful fashion in assessing progress and in determining corrective actions.

A standing committee charged with the performance oversight responsibility will benefit from the diversity of its members; the more experience, talent, expertise, and the wider and more diverse the perspectives brought to the table, the more powerful the process is likely to be. This diversity, however, should not lead to hard and fast delegations of responsibility on the committee. For example, all committee members should take collective accountability for understanding, assessing, and acting on financial performance data. They should not succumb to the natural temptation to delegate the financial piece to the committee member who happens to be a corporate chief financial officer and the only true expert-in-residence.

Requiring that all financial and programmatic performance reports are presented at full board meetings by members of the management or operations committee is a tried-and-true way to ensure that committee members truly do understand and "own" what they are reporting. No board member would want to risk the embarrassment of stumbling through an obviously ill-digested financial report.

It Begins with Planning

Stripped to its essentials, effective performance oversight involves board members, the chief executive, and executive staff in spending considerable time around the same table, reviewing and asking important questions about pertinent information on association performance, and deciding what to do, if anything, in response to identified performance problems. How deeply to look, the technology to be employed in collecting information, the analytical tools to apply, and the time and other resources to be committed to oversight are among the many design questions to which there is no one "right" answer.

An association's annual strategic and operational planning and budget cycle—more than any other factor—determines the design of its performance oversight process. Through planning, an association determines:

- its ultimate ends (its vision and mission)

- annual targets that its major operating units and programs will shoot for within its vision and mission
- action plans to achieve the targets (a schedule of work milestones on the way to the targets)
- expenditure plans (budgets) to support the action plans.

Setting Annual Performance Targets

Annual program performance targets, whether called "goals" or "objectives," and their corresponding implementation plans (basically schedule of work milestones), together comprise the meat and potatoes of a board's performance oversight process. Without a target to shoot for, how can a board judge whether progress is being made in a program or operating unit? To be useful in performance oversight, a target, whatever it is called, must be some kind of measurable outcome, rather than just an open-ended functional description.

For example, while a board might be interested in the fact that its membership services department is dedicated to growing and diversifying the association's membership, there is nothing in this commitment that can be measured, beyond the fact of any or no growth. It is impossible for a board member to determine how much growth is enough or whether it has come an at acceptable cost. By contrast, the department's membership targets for the upcoming fiscal year might include an overall increase of 15 percent in regular members and 10 percent in associate members, along with planned increases in specific subgroups, such as small business owners or minority groups.

Adding Quality and Cost to the Equation

A board's performance oversight capability can be enhanced by going beyond barebones quantitative targets and building in quality and cost parameters when the board, chief executive, and executive staff reach agreement on annual performance targets. For example, if an association's meeting and conference division plans to offer a new strategic planning series at five locations around the country, the board can easily determine after the fact whether such conferences were actually held. But the board's performance oversight will be greatly strengthened if performance standards related to such factors as net income per workshop, attendance numbers, participant composition (there may be target participant groups), and participant satisfaction are added to the plans.

Setting Strategic Targets

The reader will recall (see Chapter 9) that an association's strategic management process involves identifying strategic issues (opportunities to move toward, and barriers in the way of, the association's vision), selecting the issues that deserve attention now, and fashioning action strategies to address them. Typically, in-house task forces are used as a vehicle for the development of detailed action plans to carry out the strategies. An association board can play an important role in monitoring the implementation of these task-force plans.

For example, let's say that an association of regional and national insurance companies and local insurance agencies has identified as one of its strategic issues the absence of any growth among its national company membership. The task force established to address this issue has established as one of the key strategic initiatives increasing national company membership by 35 percent in two years. To achieve this initiative, the task force has fashioned a detailed implementation plan involving the development of a new brochure that more effectively describes company membership benefits, the beefing up of company participation in the annual trade show, and a special, one-time membership fee reduction for new company members. This association's board now has ample pegs on which to hang the performance oversight hat: the achievement, ultimately, of the 35 percent target, along with several measurable milestones along the way.

Monitoring Work in Progress

For some targets, it may be enough to know, after the fact, whether they occurred on schedule and how they measured up to planned quality and cost criteria. Then the board's assessment can be factored into next year's plan. When the stakes associated with a particular target are high enough, however, a board may want to be involved in monitoring the work being done to hit the target as it progresses. The point would be to make sure that everything is on course and that potential problems that might jeopardize achievement of the target are identified and averted.

Consider, for example, such extraordinary targets as an association's planned 75th anniversary conference, involving one of the country's preeminent corporate chief executive officers as a keynoter, twice the normal attendance, and extensive press coverage; an association's launching an entirely new product to meet new member needs; or an association's design and construction of a new headquarters building. The work being done to achieve these visible, high-stakes, high-cost targets would almost certainly merit much closer board scrutiny while it is being done than in the case of more routine targets.

Regarding the 75th anniversary conference, the association board's management or operations committee might schedule three review sessions with the conference coordinator, at which progress in achieving workplan milestones would be reviewed and major glitches addressed. For example, the keynote speaker cancels, and the committee brainstorms other possibilities and assigns responsibility for making contacts.

Financial Targets

The operational planning and budget preparation process is capable of identifying various kinds of financial performance indicators, as long as the planning process is designed to produce them. Examples include:

- associationwide revenue and expenditure targets, perhaps scheduled monthly or quarterly in addition to annual targets
- a planned ending fund balance (including specification of operating deficits to be subsidized by the association's reserves)
- revenue targets by major sources of income (such as different categories of membership fees, grants, earned income)
- program and major operating unit expenditure plans (the tried-and-true operating budget)
- more specialized information on costs and net income for various kinds of auxiliary enterprises that are expected to generate financial, bottom-line results

Overall, a board will be interested in the maintenance of the planned balance of revenue and expenditures, keeping program expenditures in line with the budget, and the "profitability" of the association's enterprises.

Reporting and Using Performance Information

An association's planning process should determine what the association needs to know to monitor performance by generating performance targets, with any associated quality and cost parameters, and corresponding work milestones. Considerable creative design work remains to be done, preferably by a standing operations or management committee of the board working closely with the chief executive and his or her top staff. Of special interest to the board are how and when information is to be reported, how performance reviews are to be conducted, and how follow-through to such reviews is to be handled.

In answering these questions, an association board will want to beware of some real and present dangers in the realm of performance oversight that can be averted by following some simple design guidelines.

Focus on Pertinent Information

More often than not, the problem with performance reporting systems is too much, rather than not enough, information. When what John Carver calls "monitoring information" is buried in an avalanche of what he terms "incidental information," then, at best, the critical information will be diluted; at worst completely obliterated. A notorious culprit is narrative accomplishments and activities reporting, which is often intended to convince a board of how hard staff are working and how much they are accomplishing. Perhaps the best example of worst practice is financial reporting, which all too often buries a board in unreadable balance-sheet information, pertinent only to the auditors, or so much nuts-and-bolts expenditure information that the important patterns are excruciatingly painful to extract.

Employ Creative Reporting Formats

Believe it or not, some boards actually find their performance oversight role both interesting and fun. In these happy instances, not only is the right information being reported, but it is also reported in such a fashion as to pique interest and to facilitate understanding. In this regard, the chief executive and his or her staff should "care enough to send the very best," going beyond merely transmitting narrative reports and experimenting with creative use of graphics and visual aids (Figures 11 and 12).

Provide Creative Analysis

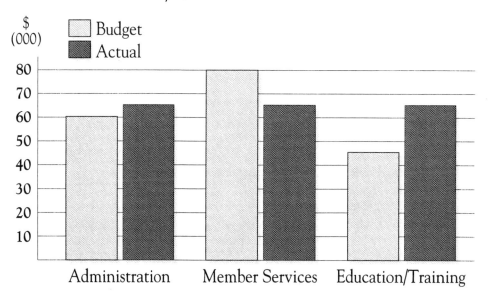

Figure 11. Monthly Financial Report: August

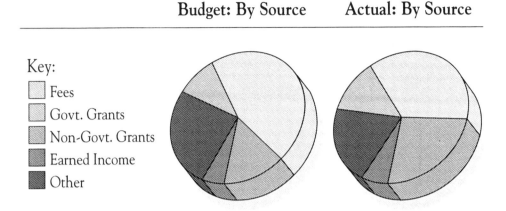

Budget: By Source   Actual: By Source

Key:
- Fees
- Govt. Grants
- Non-Govt. Grants
- Earned Income
- Other

Figure 12. End of Year Revenue Analysis

Volunteers on boards lead incredibly busy lives and have little time to devote to understanding complex information. Despite the conventional wisdom, the facts seldom do speak for themselves, at least not loudly and completely enough. Ensuring that the pertinent performance information is carefully analyzed by staff and that their analysis (conclusions, implications) is reported along with the facts is an important way to infuse more meaning into the monitoring process.

Set Aside Adequate Time for Review and Action

If the only venue for performance reporting and review is a full board meeting, whether monthly or less often, then the potential for ritualistic and perfunctory review is much greater than if a standing committee of the association board is able to devote a full meeting to discussing performance information. One technique that has proved highly productive for many associations is the quarterly or semi-annual in-depth review of program and fiscal performance. These affairs typically last for a half-day and involve meticulous staff preparation. They are structured to result in the identification of critical performance issues and in agreement on corrective actions, and are followed-up on by the preparation of written summaries of conclusions and decisions and subsequent reporting on implementation of the agreed-upon actions.

The performance information that an association board reviews on a regular basis is basically intended to indicate whether the association is on-track in carrying out its plans; hence, considerable attention is paid to important means information—what Houle calls "formative evaluation." Of course, formative evaluation does not tell a board about the ultimate impact and cost-effectiveness of association targets. Summative evaluation by definition takes place at the end of a planning year, when information of impacts and results can be gathered and analyzed. Quite often an annual strategic planning work session is an effective venue for the use of summative information, as part of an analysis of association strengths and weaknesses.

One of the design challenges for a board's management or operations committee is to determine what special information should be collected as part of the summative evaluation and how much should be spent on it. The cost can be quite high, for example, in conducting a membership satisfaction survey that covers all major programs.

Chapter Eleven
External Relations

Reaching Out

Understanding the external world—conditions, trends, and evolving membership needs and demands—is only one element of an association's comprehensive external relations strategy. Association vitality and growth depend on creating a strong, positive public image and on building and managing positive, productive relationships with groups, organizations, and institutions in the wider world, whence come:

- financial resources
- political support
- joint-venture partnerships
- regulations
- competition

The external relations arena offers a number of significant opportunities for creative board involvement for three major reasons:

1. **Ties to the Wider World**—The people who join association boards are typically active in the wider world, bringing to their board roles extensive ties with other groups and organizations.

2. **Scant Staffing**—Only a handful of the largest associations can afford to commit many staff and other resources to external relations functions. The rest depend heavily on the hands-on assistance of their board members in fashioning and carrying out external relations strategies.

3. **Reputation**—Many board members bring the reputation and prestige that can capture the attention of external audiences.

The Power of Image

A clear, positive public image can be a powerful tool for association development and growth. It ensures that an association's legitimate accomplishments are recognized and credited, fosters membership growth, attracts financial resources, and generates public support.

On the other hand, an association that allows its image to be unfocused or, worse, to erode, may find its good works unappreciated and its support waning. Indeed, savvy association board members and executives treat image as one of their association's most precious assets: to be developed with great care, to be nurtured and cherished, and to be guarded against assault. They know that, while strong images can see associations through rocky periods, they are also notoriously fragile, capable of being tarnished overnight in today's world of pervasive, rapid electronic communication.

A Special Committee

In light of the importance of image building and external relations, and the opportunities for in-depth board involvement, an association board should consider creating a standing external relations committee. In addition to overseeing the association's development and implementation of external relations strategies, this committee might coordinate board members' hands-on contributions. Staff responsible for association public relations, legislative relations, and marketing should work closely with this committee.

In light of the potential for hands-on board participation in the external relations arena, it will make sense for the external relations committee to consist of board members professionally involved in public relations, marketing, and the media, as well as members who are involved in several other organizations.

Board Roles

Association boards can play an active role in ensuring that their associations are seen by the wider world as they want to be seen by:

Creating an Image Vision—The number one job is to ensure that one of the major outcomes of an association's strategic management process is an updated image vision that spells out clearly and in detail how the association wants to be viewed by its key audiences (see Chapter 9). To be of any use in shaping external relations strategy, the image vision should be highly detailed. The reader should keep in mind that an abbreviated version can always be crafted for public consumption.

Identifying Image Gaps—The field of external relations is filled with conventional wisdom about what works and what doesn't. To ensure that an association's external relations strategies yield the highest feasible return on the association's investment, it is essential that the association understand what issues it needs to tackle. In this context, a strategic issue is a gap between an element of the image vision and how the association is actually seen by a key audience. For example, a segment of the membership might be surveyed to determine whether they really do see the association as inclusive and welcoming, customer-responsive, and preoccupied with quality. Major gaps can be targeted for special attention.

Planning and Committing Resources—Another key board job is to make sure that, through the operational planning and budget preparation process, an association builds the capability to promote its image—that external relations targets are set, plans are fashioned, and resources are budgeted. One of a board's key responsibilities is to ensure that the operational plans and budgets of association operating units and programs not only reinforce the desired image, but also that they in no way counteract it. This check can be built into the annual board-staff operational planning work session (see Chapter 9).

Taking a Hands-On Role—An association board can reach agreement with its chief executive officer on hands-on roles that it might play to promote a stronger image and effective public relations. For example, board members can speak on behalf of their association in important forums. These presentations will be more effective if the forums are carefully selected and if board members receive strong support in playing this role. Providing them with an attractive slide presentation, speaking outlines, and informative hand-outs, for example, will help them prepare for this role. Board members might also participate in legislative briefings and hearings, serve as advocates to funding sources, such as foundations, and keep in touch with important stakeholder organizations.

Stakeholder Management

No association, no matter how large, successful, well staffed and handsomely funded, can truly "go it alone." In today's world creative diplomacy and partnership building are essential capabilities. And so what we call "stakeholder management" has become a critical part of association management. Stakeholders are groups, organizations, and institutions in an association's environment that have a potential or actual significant influence on the association's vision, mission, strategies, plans, and operations. Stakeholders are worth maintaining a relationship with because of this influence. The higher the stakes involved in a relationship, the more attention it deserves from the association.

Membership at the Top of the List

An association's members are its preeminent stakeholder, and they typically receive considerable attention; their needs and their satisfaction with services are regularly surveyed and their participation in association affairs is well planned and monitored. However, relationships with other association stakeholders are often managed casually, as in periodic chief executive lunches, or purely on a squeaky-wheel basis, and these relationships consequently seldom fulfill their potential.

Two Stakeholder Tiers

An association's stakeholders tend to divide into two broad categories:

1. **Top-Tier Stakeholders**—Top-tier stakeholders have a continuing relationship with an association that involves significant stakes, and so an association will want to devote considerable time to building and maintaining effective relationships with them. In addition to the obvious top-tier stakeholder—an association's membership—are key congressional committees that make policy affecting an association; federal and state regulatory bodies that can impact an association's activities; other associations in the same general field, perhaps competing for the same members; and major funding sources, such as foundations.

2. **Second-Tier Stakeholders**—Second-tier stakeholders come and go, receiving serious attention only when their involvement is essential for implementing particular strategies or for resolving one problem or another. These ad hoc stakeholders are normally identified when strategies are fashioned and operational plans are developed.

Stakeholder relationships tend to be most productive when:

- they are based on a detailed understanding of the stakes involved in a relationship
- the stakeholders themselves are well understood
- detailed stakeholder management strategies are fashioned
- board and staff members take clear accountability for maintaining the relationships
- the effectiveness of the strategies is formally monitored by the board

Exploring Stakeholder Relationships

An annual board-staff strategic work session (see Chapter 9) is an ideal time for an association to explore its stakeholder relationships. A breakout group might, for example, identify key stakeholders and the stakes involved in each relationship, attempt to understand each stakeholder better, and assess the current status of each relationship. Using a kind of quid pro quo assessment, a breakout group might identify precisely what the association needs and wants from the stakeholder and what the stakeholder needs and wants in return from the association (Figure 13).

At stake can be financial resources, political support, regulation, competition, and joint venture partnerships. A single stakeholder relationship may involve diverse stakes. For example, a competitor may also be an important potential joint-venture partner.

HIDA FOUNDATION

HIDA wants diversification of its financial resources and support for education and research; the Foundation wants clear directions from HIDA and more associate members.

ASSOCIATES

HIDA wants support for distribution system and financial support; the Associates want access to membership and information.

SERVICE CORPORATION

HIDA wants revenue-generating products; the corporation wants HIDA support to build its entrepreneurial capacity.

DEALER BUYING GROUPS

HIDA wants to retain members, to merge shows, and not to contend with competition; the Buying Groups want to tap into HIDA resources and to make money on programs.

CONGRESS

HIDA wants influence on policy; Congress wants PAC contributions and information for policy formulation.

Figure 13. Stakeholder Analysis

Understanding Stakeholders

The better a key stakeholder is understood, the more effective any strategies fashioned to manage the relationship are likely to be. Stakeholders can be better understood by looking at their:

- values, vision, mission, strategies, and plans
- resources (budget, staff)
- capabilities
- track record
- political clout and reputation
- internal culture
- attitude toward the association

If, for example, an association is considering a joint venture with another association (a stakeholder), it must approach this initiative knowing whether the stakeholder association's values, vision, and mission will accommodate the venture; whether the potential partner brings sufficient resources to the table to be an attractive partner; and the association's track record in implementing similar initiatives is solid. It must also know how to approach the association—understanding its culture includes understanding its diplomatic and decision making processes. Proceeding to develop the venture without this knowledge base would truly be a high-risk affair.

Stakeholder Management Strategies

Association boards that have gone through a stakeholder identification and analysis process in a retreat setting have been amazed at the number of top-tier stakeholders they identify. A list of 30 to 40 is not at all uncommon. On the face of it, the chief executive alone, or even the chief executive and his or her staff, cannot possibly pay detailed attention to all of even the most important stakeholders all of the time. The key to success is to map out the key elements or steps involved in managing each relationship and to assign specific accountabilities for each element.

The highest priority stakeholders might be involved in important ways in an association's internal affairs. For example, key stakeholders might be invited to join an association's board, or they might participate in an association's annual board-staff strategic work session. Not only do stakeholders bring to an association valuable information and new perspectives on issues, but their participation also enlarges the potential for partnerships by deepening understanding of each other and by exploring joint-venture opportunities. Time and again, association boards have found that interacting with stakeholders in retreat settings is a powerful way to correct erroneous assumptions about stakeholder aims and attitudes and to lower barriers of suspicion and distrust. Such a setting can also enable participants to resolve long-standing conflicts that have defied solution at a distance.

Far less dramatic but nonetheless useful are such steps as putting key stakeholders on an association's mailing list, inviting them to participate in association conferences, and being willing to promote their interests by, for example, publicizing their meetings and conferences in association publications.

The Board's Role

Board members can play a strong, creative role in stakeholder relationship management, and, indeed, they must in the case of associations with limited staff. Among the more important roles are:

- Serving as the formal liaison person to a particular association. This role might involve keeping in touch with the stakeholder by regularly reviewing its publications and attending its annual conference, keeping the association board apprised of opportunities and problems in the relationship.
- Taking a lead-role in working through a particular problem or capitalizing on a major opportunity, such as a possible merger of two associations.
- Perhaps even serving on the stakeholder's board, provided that this can be done without any conflict of interest.

Affiliated Foundations

In the wider nonprofit world, boards often play a significant role in generating financial resources, and many have a standing resource development committee. Nonprofit board members contribute dollars, head capital campaigns, fashion donor strategies, and make personal contacts with potential donors and funding sources such as foundations.

Associations often establish affiliated 501(c)(3) organizations with their own boards for the purpose of fund raising. While this makes good sense, such foundations sometimes operate largely independently of their parent associations. They have been known to set their own funding priorities, thereby actually shaping the parent association's strategies rather than responding to them. And some have funded and operated their own programs outside of the parent association's organizational structure.

To ensure that such foundations directly support their parent associations, their fund-raising and grant-making activities must be driven by their parent association's priorities, strategies, plans, and needs. The point is to ensure that the association's needs are met, not vice versa. One approach that has worked is to formally involve a foundation board in the parent association's planning process. At the very least, the parent association can formally communicate its funding priorities to its foundation board.

Section IV

Retreats, Change Management, and Sources

Chapter Twelve

Running Top-Notch Retreats

Horror Tales Abound

It seems like every other association has its favorite horror tale of retreats gone awry, leaving a bad taste in participants' mouths—and a strong resistance to future get-togethers. Some I hear most frequently:

The Editing Experience—We spent the whole morning laboring over a one-paragraph mission statement, debating particular phraseology—even specific words. Talk about boring! You could just feel the enthusiasm oozing away, and we had so many important issues to grapple with. It felt kind of like being back in English 101. We did get a carefully crafted paragraph, but I've never sweated so much to produce so little, so painfully, in my life. So don't come to us again soon talking about the need for a retreat.

The Illusion of Precision—We brainstormed for a couple of hours in break-out groups, looking at really important things going on outside the association—you know, new legislation, sweeping population shifts, exciting new technologies—and making a list of what seemed to be the most important issues facing the association. We were excited about getting a handle on some truly important matters and really preparing the association to get ahead of the game and moving beyond this feeling of being overwhelmed by events.

But then the retreat leader insisted that we go through a rinky-dink exercise of voting on the top issues, I guess so we would feel that we had actually decided something. So we were all given little green, red, blue, and yellow sticky-dots representing different weights, and we spent what seemed like ages voting on the relative importance of each issue. What a waste of time! Everyone knew that the issues needed a lot more study and discussion before we decided the ones that really needed attention. To vote by the seat of our pants only made the whole thing *seem* more scientific.

Problem Overload—Don't ask me how it happened, but we somehow got on the track of working through all of the problems that we saw in the association during our very long day together. I guess the idea was to cut through the you-know-what, digging into the gut things and not wasting time fantasizing about the future—that sort of macho approach. All we had at the end were long lists of the pros and cons about all kinds of issues, everything from strategy to loose screws three echelons down. We left tired, beaten down, and depressed by all the problems. We just never knew how many things weren't going well.

The Touchy-Feely Glow—Things had been so tense for so long—board members nit-picking staff recommendations to death, staff getting more and more defensive, lots of quibbling among board members. So it seemed like a great idea to spend a day or so clearing the air and rebuilding the leadership team. We found a top-notch trainer type with lots of experience in team building and went off to a lovely state lodge for an overnight. It was really fun and interesting. We got to know each other much better, and I don't mean just on the surface. We learned powerful ways to go deeper inside to know ourselves better. We left feeling renewed—there was a real warm glow of, almost, friendship. But that was six weeks ago, and board meetings are quickly becoming as tense as ever, staff have clammed up again, nothing's changed. I still think touching and feeling are good, but the effect sure doesn't last long.

The Cookie Cutter—We knew we needed to spend some extended time together, thinking about the kinds of fundamental questions that never survive the day-to-day pressures, and so we found a trainer with impressive credentials to lead the retreat. What a commandant she was! She had this process that had apparently worked lots of places. We started with everyone filling out this elaborate questionnaire for the first couple of hours, and then we tabulated the results and discussed what we wanted to focus on that afternoon. The trouble was that half our group was so turned off by the morning that they skipped out after lunch. We kept going, and did produce something, but it didn't really mean much with half the group gone. Two things really bother me about the experience. First, our facilitator should have picked up the tension early in the day and worked with us to restructure. No chance, though. Her approach was the way to go. And I'm sorry that we didn't get involved in planning the retreat. We shouldn't have just left it to the "expert."

Powerful Potential Nonetheless

The reader will surely relate to one or more of these tales of woe, and can probably add several others. But, despite their misuse and abuse, retreats can be an effective association vehicle for producing powerful results. The basic idea is sound, but the execution is often faulty, and so retreats have earned a bad reputation. The idea, of course, is to set aside at least a day away from the shop to deal with matters that require intensive, sustained attention that do not lend themselves to a quick fix. The prior chapters of this book have identified a number of occasions when a well-planned and executed board-staff retreat can produce powerful results for an association. Retreats are especially effective vehicles for providing boards with an opportunity to provide essential top-down guidance and to "jump-start" ongoing processes, for example:

- fashioning an association board's leadership design (see Chapter 3)
- kicking off strategic planning by updating an association's vision and mission and identifying strategic issues to tackle (Chapter 9)

- guiding the preparation of the budget by reaching detailed agreement on operational planning targets and resolving operational policy questions (Chapter 9)

Many association boards and their chief executives have used retreats successfully to produce these and other important results. The keys are clear design and meticulous execution.

Some Golden Rules

Association boards and chief executives considering a retreat should take seriously the lessons that successful experience offers:

1. Involve board members in the development of a clear retreat design.
2. Ensure that board members actively participate in leading the retreat.
3. Communicate the design well in advance to all invited participants.
4. Diversify retreat attendance to the extent feasible.
5. Build in systematic follow-through.

Ad Hoc Retreat Design Committee

A sensible first step in putting together a successful retreat is for an association board chair to appoint an ad hoc committee to put the retreat design together. Typically headed by the board chair and consisting of the chief executive officer and two to five board members, the ad hoc committee need meet only once, for approximately a half-day, to accomplish its job. There is no need for only retreat "champions" to serve on the ad hoc retreat design committee. If an influential board member has raised questions about the value of a retreat, it might make good sense for this internal critic to be involved in putting it together. Otherwise, he or she may continue sniping away from the sidelines.

The agenda of the ad hoc committee's single meeting will be to put the detailed design of the upcoming retreat together, for the purpose of ensuring *that retreat participants achieve everything they intend to achieve within the time allotted.* As a result of the front-end design process, the risks that the retreat will produce unintended negative results, dash participants' expectations, break-down midstream, or actually do more harm than good can be minimized.

Design involves answering in detail certain key questions:

1. What outcomes do we want to achieve during our time together?
2. What structure do we want to employ to facilitate achievement of the outcomes?
3. How much time do we need to spend together to achieve these outcomes? Will an overnight make sense?

4. What agenda makes sense in light of the identified outcomes and the structure we intend to employ?
5. What kind of location makes sense?
6. What board members should play leadership roles in the retreat and how can we prepare them to play these roles?
7. What staff members should attend and how should they participate?
8. What nonboard and nonstaff members should be invited to attend?
9. How should follow-up be handled to ensure that the retreat produces powerful, enduring results, rather than becoming a not-so-fond memory?

Deciding on Technical Assistance

As they think about holding a retreat, association board members will early on, even before putting together the design committee, need to decide whether to employ a professional third-party facilitator to assist in designing and running the retreat. In addition to the obvious advantage of specialized expertise and tested experience, a professional retreat facilitator is typically granted more latitude to raise tough and sensitive questions because he or she is perceived as politically neutral and unswayed by vested interests.

Deciding whether to employ a professional prior to getting the ad hoc retreat committee going will make sense for two reasons. First, the more involved in creating the design, the more effective a third-party facilitator is likely to be. And second, a professional facilitator can provide strong assistance to the ad hoc committee, including facilitation and follow-up. For example, a professional facilitator might make design recommendations, drawing on interviews with board members and the chief executive; review of pertinent association documentation, such as board minutes and the current strategic plan and budget; and experience in running retreats.

In selecting a third-party facilitator, an association board will want to consider such factors as:

- experience in working with similar groups in producing related results
- in-depth expertise, such as in board development or strategic planning
- style, keeping in mind that not every style fits every group equally well
- methodologies, in terms of their fit with the group and the facilitator's flexibility in tailoring them to specific groups

Outcomes

What an association wants to achieve should drive every other element of a retreat design, and the outcomes will be more valuable as they are more specific and measurable. A guiding rule for the ad hoc retreat design committee in determining outcomes should be: to capitalize on our time together, achieving as much as we feasibly can at the quality we want. The feasibility factor is critical: The retreat should be well enough designed that it is clearly manageable and the possibility of break-down is remote. One of the most important benefits of a third-party facilitator is to recommend outcomes to the ad hoc retreat design committee, based on her or his research on association needs.

Direct Content

Outcomes tend to divide into two main groups: direct content outcomes and less direct process-spin-offs. Content outcomes relate to products that can be seen, read, held. For example, in the area of strategic planning, content outcomes are values, vision, and mission statements; environmental trends and conditions reviews; assessments of strengths; strategic issues; and action strategies. Relative to board leadership development, the preeminent content outcome would be a board leadership design, and more specific content outcomes would include an association board's leadership mission, its standing committee structure, and its meeting schedule, among others. A board-staff operational planning retreat might focus on such content outcomes as major operating unit performance targets for the coming year and policies to address identified operational issues.

Process Spin-Offs

It is not uncommon to find situations where an association stands to gain as much from producing less direct, intangible process-spin-offs as the more easily recognizable direct products. At the very least, they tend to be very important. For example, an association may see an upcoming retreat as a powerful means for:

- building a stronger board-staff culture, characterized by a deeper understanding of each other and greater mutual respect
- strengthening the leadership skills of participants by going through a challenging process that tests and stretches participants
- identifying board members who can be brought along to positions of greater responsibility on the board

- making everyone feel better about their roles by providing them with fun and relaxation
- building the ownership of outcomes through creative and meaningful participation
- strengthening relationships with key stakeholders of the association

Structure

Retreat structure is basically the organization of the time that participants will spend together. A fundamental design question that must be answered early on is the extent to which the retreat is to be structured along presentation and reaction lines as opposed to involving participants in creating and generating information. The ad hoc design group should keep in mind that retreats involving considerable formal presentation and the introduction of pounds of paper tend to dampen participation, quell interest, and, worst of all, stifle creativity. A good working rule is to keep formal presentation to an absolute minimum. If, for example, one of the desired products is a vision statement, participants should create the statement, not merely review a draft statement. Don't forget that the board's planning committee can always clean it up and refine it after the retreat, so messiness need not be of concern.

Breakout Groups

Structuring participation is also quite important. A very small retreat group (say, six or fewer) may decide to spend all of the time in plenary session, but the more participants involved, the more important the use of breakout groups becomes. If well structured, breakout groups can produce significant benefits in a board-staff retreat. Not only can more ideas and questions be generated in the time available, but also participants will have more opportunity to contribute, making the meeting more fun for them and increasing their ownership of the results. Large group participation tends to dampen participation and to encourage natural performers to shine at the expense of more reticent participants.

For example, a strategic planning retreat involving fifteen participants might employ a total of six breakout groups in three rounds with two breakout groups meeting concurrently in each round:

Round 1: the vision group; the mission group

Round 2: the trends and conditions group; the internal strengths and weaknesses group

Round 3: the products and customers issues group; the image and public relations issues group

Ensuring Productivity

An ad hoc retreat design committee planning to employ breakout groups in its upcoming retreat can ensure the groups are productive by paying special attention to:

Fashioning Clear Guidelines—Fashioning clear guidelines for each group, describing what it is to produce during the retreat and the process it will follow. For example, one of the most productive approaches for generating significant content and fully involving people is free-flowing brainstorming with no "right" or "wrong" answers. This approach does not seek consensus or formal decisions; rather, it produces content that requires further refinement, either in plenary session or subsequent to the retreat.

Selecting and Assisting Leaders—Carefully selecting breakout group leaders and providing them with assistance in carrying out their roles. In addition to making sure that breakout group leaders are as diverse as feasible (in gender, age, experience, race, viewpoints), their skills, knowledge, and expressed interests should be taken into account in assigning them to particular groups. It would, for example, be quite unwise to assign a rat-a-tat-tat, nuts-and-bolts type who has frequently talked about vision as a flaky concept to head the vision breakout group. Assistance might include: an orientation session for breakout group leaders, a tip sheet on how to run breakout groups, and written background information pertinent to the topic a group is assigned to address (for example, trends and conditions data for the trends group, or the most recent financial report for the strengths and weaknesses group).

Assigning Participants—Carefully assigning participants to breakout groups, taking into account their interests and knowledge, and the chemistry involved in different combinations of people.

Organizing Presentations—Requiring that all members of a break-out group stand at the front of the room in plenary session and every group member participates in reporting, rather than relying on the group chair or a designated reporter. This will keep all participants' attention focused during the break-out group session (lest a point be missed), build ownership of the reports, and let everyone share in the limelight.

Break-out group reporting can add fun and spice to a meeting by experimenting with different reporting formats. For example, groups have, on the spot, written skits and rap tunes, employed talk-show formats, and even created rough and ready props. One group constructed a paper coffin, which it carried out while humming a few bars of Chopin's Funeral March to symbolize an outmoded policy calling for immediate change.

The Agenda

The purpose of a blow-by-blow agenda is to schedule key retreat steps within the framework of the structure. It ensures that they move forward in logical order and that enough time is allocated to carry out each step fully, but that the pace is rapid enough to maintain momentum and build interest. For example, should the first major event of a strategic planning retreat be a slide presentation by the facilitator on the strategic planning process? If so, how much time should be allocated to such a briefing? Or would it be better to jump immediately into an exercise, such as visioning, as a way to capture interest and build enthusiasm early on? How long should the first round of break-out groups last? And how much time should each group have for reporting and discussion in the plenary session that follows each break-out round?

No one can be certain whether the time allotted to a retreat event will be too little or too much, so the flexibility to do on-the-spot agenda revision is essential. A capable third-party facilitator will be alert to the need for such revisions as a retreat progresses.

The ad hoc design committee should resist the natural temptation to schedule retreat time in the evening after a full day of work, as a way of reducing the amount of time that volunteer board members must take from work and family. The fact is, the work being done in a serious retreat is inevitably demanding, both intellectually and emotionally, and to schedule a session from 7 to 10 in the evening—after a full day of work and dinner—is guaranteed to reduce productivity at best, and, worse, to lead to low-quality deliberations.

Attendance Issues

One way to enhance the impact of a retreat is to expand attendance, regardless of the subject matter. Exclusiveness is a vastly overrated virtue. In the realm of strategy, increasing participation is a way to bring more knowledge and diverse perspectives, as well as expand the potential for partnership building. And it is probably a waste of time to work on board staff relations without the key staff present.

What is the ideal size of a retreat? There is none. All we can say is that the larger the attendance, the more attention that will have to be paid to structure, agenda, and logistics to keep the event from falling apart. I have seen retreats with more than fifty participants that, despite seeming at points like a three-ring circus, achieve powerful results and provide participants with a lot of fun to boot.

Staff Involvement

Involving as many of the key staff as feasible is almost always a good idea, and certainly in retreats involving strategic and operational planning, and board leadership design. Staff members inevitably bring essential knowledge and valuable perspectives, based on their devoting full time to association affairs. A retreat is obviously one of the best ways for boards and staff to become better acquainted and to gain a fuller appreciation for each other's roles and responsibilities, since the suspension of normal communication rules inevitably leads to fuller, less guarded communication. And by interacting with their board in a retreat setting, staff can learn ways to work more effectively with the board.

Stakeholder Involvement

Association boards can also make their retreats more productive by inviting key stakeholder organizations to send representatives. The reader will recall that a stakeholder is any group, organization, or institution in an association's environment with actual or potential significant influence on the association's planning and operations. Of course, the greater the potential influence, the higher the stakes, and hence the greater the importance of maintaining an effective relationship with the stakeholder. The stakes involved in any stakeholder relationship can be very positive (financial and political support, joint venture partnership) and negative (competition for the same members or customers).

By inviting important stakeholders to a strategic planning retreat, an association can tap their knowledge, expertise, and wisdom. Diversifying attendance by including stakeholders is also an important way to strengthen working relationships and to identify opportunities for creative collaboration, such as joint-venturing an innovative new program or joining forces in going for a foundation grant.

Dirty-Laundry Concerns

Since stakeholders are, by definition, "outsiders," an ad hoc retreat design committee may well worry about the danger of "washing dirty laundry" outside the "family." Experience has taught that the danger is minimal and the fear always exaggerated. A meticulously designed retreat can restrain any tendencies toward self-flagellation, but even if a filthy sock or two is exposed, who cares? Opening a retreat to key stakeholders is a way to display an association board's fundamental self-confidence, as well as telling the stakeholders that we really do value their opinion.

All invited nonboard members, whether staff or outside stakeholders, should be encouraged to participate freely and fully in all retreat deliberations, with no status differentiation. It is especially important that staff come to the table—within the retreat framework—as equals, expected not to support deliberations, but to be fully engaged in them.

Setting and Set-Up

The basic locational requirement is to be in a reasonably comfortable and attractive setting free of day-to-day business distractions. If the budget allows, a more bucolic location with ample recreational opportunities can both heighten enjoyment and stimulate the flow of creative juices. And staying overnight can add a whole dimension to a retreat, providing far more opportunity for board members, staff, and stakeholders to interact casually than a 9 to 5 framework can.

Associations tempted to be tight-fisted should keep in mind that retreats are rare occurrences whose costs can be amortized over a long period, they involve the most influential leaders in the association, and they deal with issues of tremendous importance. Where high stakes affairs such as a retreat are concerned, to be penny-wise is surely to be pound-foolish.

The plenary session set-up that appears to work best is tables arranged horseshoe fashion. Members are seated around the perimeter with board members, staff, and stakeholder representatives well interspersed. Casual resort dress also helps to promote collegiality and to break down formal barriers.

Communicating the Design

When the ad hoc retreat design committee has put all of the retreat design elements in place, it makes sense to pull them together in a comprehensive written description that can be transmitted in memorandum form to all invited participants, preferably at least a month before the retreat. Co-signed by the committee chair, the chief executive officer, and the professional facilitator (if one was used), this description should cover in detail (say, five to eight pages) the:

- retreat design assumptions, explaining why the retreat has been scheduled
- outcomes to be tackled
- structure—describing each of the break-out groups that will be used in terms of what they are to produce and the methodologies to be used
- blow-by-blow agenda

Mailing out the comprehensive retreat agenda well in advance of the event will serve two major purposes: (1) it will explain exactly what will happen, aligning participants' expectations and allaying any fears (as in, What in heaven's name will happen to me?); and (2) it will serve to stimulate attendance, by making clear how ambitious and well organized the meeting will be, and, often, how different it will be from whatever negative retreat experiences some of the invited participants have had in the past.

Follow-Through

The ad hoc retreat design committee can ensure that a board-staff retreat is not an end in itself and that enduring results are produced, by building into the retreat design:

- explicit ties to ongoing association process, for example, making the annual strategic planning retreat the kick-off event of a full-blown strategic management process
- production of a detailed report that covers all of the major points and decisions made during the retreat, and, if desired, recommends follow-through action
- detailed review of the retreat report by all participants as soon after the retreat as possible to confirm the decisions and to agree on next steps

Taking the strategic planning example, an association might follow up on its annual strategic session by: having the board's planning committee refine any vision and mission statements developed and recommend board adoption; establishing task forces to fashion detailed action strategies to address strategic issues identified at the retreat; and communicating priorities to guide the soon-to-begin operational planning process.

Implementing change is such a challenging process that it is discussed in detail in the following chapter.

Chapter Thirteen
Implementing Change

The Metropolis Chamber's Retreat

Let us suppose that the board and executive team of the fictional Metropolis Chamber of Commerce, which we first met in Chapter 2, spent one-and-a-half days together at a nearby conference center, hammering out new chamber strategies during the first day and concentrating on a new board leadership design the next half-day. There was near-unanimous agreement among the retreat participants that significant changes in chamber board structure and process would be essential over the coming year if the board was to provide the chamber with the foresightful and proactive leadership required for future growth and fiscal stability. Everyone agreed that the board had become so driven from the bottom-up by numerous program committees and task forces (downtown development, education, the port) that overall chamber corporate directions were almost completely absent.

Change Initiatives Identified

Recognizing the urgent need for stronger board leadership, retreat participants identified a number of critical changes that needed to be made over the coming eighteen months or so, chief among them:

- diversifying the board's membership by adding more small business and minority members
- upgrading the board member nominating process to ensure that new members fit a detailed profile of attributes and qualifications
- providing for the development and enforcement of board member performance standards, via a reconstituted executive committee that was to focus on coordinating board operations rather than on being a petite board-within-the-board
- replacing the monthly board meeting with a bimonthly meeting, which was to become quarterly within a year
- establishing four, new, broadly functional governance committees to replace nine program-focused committees: planning and business development; operational oversight; external relations and resource development; and membership

- significantly upgrading the board's role in strategic and operational planning, basically through the detailed design and implementation of a new planning cycle

This ambitious change agenda was unanimously confirmed at a follow-up session three weeks after the retreat, when the retreat facilitator presented his report, summarizing all of the key points and decisions made during the retreat. Two of the three key elements of the chamber's program to upgrade its board leadership were now in place: knowledge of what to do and the desire to do it. The third—*how to accomplish the change*—also had to be tackled if the planned improvements were actually to be made.

Managing Change

Intents and commitments are words on paper; translating them into actual practice is always a challenge—for both individuals and organizations. To ensure that today's intents do not become tomorrow's not-so-fond memories requires that people and organizations pay close attention to the meticulous planning and execution involved in moving from words to action.

No matter how daunting the challenge may have appeared, our fictional Metropolis Chamber really had no choice. The only realistic alternative to embracing, directing, and guiding change, in the light of an evolving mission and changing circumstances was to be changed by external forces. Change is a constant these days. The question every person and organization must answer is whether he, she, or it intends to change, voluntarily and with some measure of control, or to be changed. So, what could the Metropolis Chamber of Commerce to do to ensure that its huge investment of time and energy in fashioning the change agenda ultimately yielded a substantial return to the chamber? The first step was to understand the nature of the challenge.

Barriers to Overcome

Despite all of the pep talks these days in pop psychology, planned, systematic, large-scale change tends not to happen. The odds, sad to say, are against it. Why is change so difficult? Three barriers loom largest on the nonprofit association landscape:

1. **Need for Sustained Time and Attention**—Significant change takes sustained time and attention that are normally not given. Once the warm glow of a retreat has dimmed, life in the trench of day-to-day operations has a way of overwhelming good intentions. Phones jangle, in-baskets fill, crises clamor for immediate attention, energies wane, focus is diluted, change fades away. The reader should never underestimate how inexorable an association's day-to-day demands can be and how fragile planned change always is. Inertia is the inevitable default winner, unless concerted action is taken to combat it.

2. **Normal Human Resistance**—Many, if not most, human beings resist change, even if they are not consciously aware of it. Change has no natural constituency, while allegiance to the known, the familiar, and the comfortable can be quite strong. Change, no matter how well planned, takes people into unknown terrain, raising all kinds of fears. Well, today may not be all that great, but couldn't tomorrow be a lot worse? Can I measure up to new demands? Will I fail and look inept, or even worse, silly? I have found my niche, which makes me feel like I'm contributing in some important way, but where will I be in the new structure? A nobody, after all this work? Not on your life! Such normal resistance is all the more insidious when it is made to appear rational. For example, how often has the reader seen valuable initiatives scuttled by something I call "killing change with a million sensible questions," or by another pathology known as "needing to know every possible consequence in advance"?

3. **No Shelter**—A change agenda often has no organizational home to protect and nurture it, and to keep it in the forefront of an association's collective consciousness. Without a home, and bereft of protection, planned change can literally fade out of collective consciousness and thus out of existence. We lose track of it because it is not part of mainstream association management routines.

Beating the Odds

Hoping that the reader is not too depressed by the bad news that planned and guided change is very hard to do, I am pleased to share the good: There are practical, affordable ways that a committed association board, its chief executive, and management team can employ to keep their change agenda from being overwhelmed by normal human resistance and the demands of day-to-day operations. The change management guidelines that follow are based on the successful experience of hundreds of nonprofit boards in fashioning and carrying out change agendas and from the rapidly developing field of change management. The reader interested in pursuing the subject can now draw on a spate of books on managing change—especially on the powerful work of Rosabeth Moss-Kanter, whose *When Giants Learn to Dance* is a classic in the field.

Four broad guidelines will enable an association board and chief executive to beat the odds in directing and managing their change agendas:

1. Create a special structure or program to manage change.

A change agenda must be protected, nurtured, led, and managed with explicit roles, accountabilities, and processes. Merely tossing the change agenda into the maelstrom of daily events is the best way of making sure nothing happens; it will inevitably be sucked under, disappearing from sight and eventually from mind, too. The reader will know that all is not well with change when it becomes just another agenda item at the regular board or executive team meetings.

A practical alternative to the sink-or-swim approach is to create a special, ad hoc association program explicitly dedicated to implementing the change agenda that has been developed. In the Metropolis Chamber case, this would mean, during the current year, implementing a number of board upgrading initiatives, including four new standing committees.

This special change structure or program can be given an appropriate name, such as strategic organizational development program, and provided with staff support (typically not new staff, but as an added responsibility of existing staff). As basically an ad hoc organization within the association administrative structure, this change program can provide the focus and sustained attention required to implement the change agenda.

2. Ensure continuing board ownership.

By virtue of its participation in the retreat that generated the change initiatives aimed at strengthening its leadership, the Metropolis Chamber of Commerce board already felt considerable ownership of the change agenda. This ownership must be sustained and even strengthened as the weeks and months pass to ensure timely implementation of the agenda. The minute that the chamber board begins to think of the agenda as theirs (the staff's), rather than ours (the board's and staff's), essential vital energy has been lost and will be extremely hard to restore.

3. Keep the chief executive officer in the forefront.

As the highest-ranking, full-time, paid professional in the association, the chief executive makes or breaks a change program regardless of his or her board's intent and commitment. Just by publicly signaling a lack of passion for change, the chief executive will shake confidence in the planned change, thereby eroding faith and commitment. And by spending less time on directing and supporting the change effort, the chief executive can significantly slow progress.

To ensure that the change initiatives are carried out, the chief executive must be—in word and action—the officer-in-charge of change. He or she must be its most visible and passionate advocate, not just its grudging supporter. He or she must provide clear direction to staff in supporting the change effort, and he or she must devote significant time and attention to the operation of the change program.

4. Plan for Implementation in Chewable Bites

Association boards are comprised of part-time volunteers who typically lead extraordinarily busy lives, and the chief executive and staff easily fill up a 40-hour week, and usually much more, just keeping the operation going. So do we just blithely add on several more hours a month for managing the board's change agenda, without any thought to its impact? Not unless we want to see the change program come crashing down, the victim of wild-eyed wishful thinking.

The principle of "doability" is all-important in managing change. Change initiatives should be meticulously planned and carefully paced so that they can be implemented without placing undue strain on the association or jeopardizing its ongoing programs and services. Our hypothetical Metropolis Chamber of Commerce board has, let us assume, exercised generally effective leadership for nearly a half-century without the recommended new standing committees and the other planned board leadership enhancements. Surely nothing will be lost if implementation is spread over 18 months or even a couple of years, just as long as the pace is not so slow that momentum is totally lost. There is no "right" pace in managing change—just the pace that will get the job done fully in a reasonable period of time without overtaxing the association.

Key Design Elements

Once an association board, chief executive officer, and executive team have reviewed the report on their retreat, reached agreement on the change initiatives that will comprise their change agenda over the next year, and decided to create a change program to manage implementation of the changes, it's time to design a detailed change program that addresses four key design elements. These four elements are drawn from the real-life experience of hundreds of nonprofits that have successfully led and managed large-scale change programs:

- establishment of the change program's legitimacy
- development of an ad hoc policy body to oversee the change program
- assignment of a staff person to support the change program
- preparation of a comprehensive action plan to guide implementation of the change program

Establishing Program Legitimacy

If the organization within the association that is charged to carry out the planned changes is to succeed, it must be widely recognized as a legitimate part of the association. There can be no implication that a group of ambitious change champions have taken it upon themselves to run with the ball. One tested way to confer legitimacy is to have the board pass two key resolutions after it has reviewed the retreat report:

- the first, adopting the board's leadership mission that was fashioned during the retreat
- the second, establishing the change program and authorizing an ad hoc policy body to commence with preparation and execution of a comprehensive action plan to carry out the key changes

As Exhibit A shows, the resolution need go no further than generally accepting the action initiatives and authorizing the policy body (the steering committee) to fashion detailed plans. It can make clear that the full board will review and approve the comprehensive plan, will be consulted regularly during the implementation process, and will make all the decisions it would normally be expected to make relative to implementation steps (for example, to review and approve a bylaws change enabling the new committees to be created).

Providing for Policy Direction

Many associations that have successfully implemented change through a formal change program have found that creating a steering committee to direct and oversee the program works well. Usually chaired by a senior member of the board and consisting of three to five board members, the chief executive officer, and the board chair (ex officio), the sole purpose of this ad hoc steering committee is to serve as the policy body of the change program in these capacities:

- reviewing the retreat report line-by-line and establishing implementation priorities
- overseeing development of, reviewing, and recommending board adoption of the change program comprehensive action plan
- overseeing implementation of the action plan, and monitoring and reporting progress to the full board
- ensuring that any board or wider membership policy decisions (such as bylaws revision) needed to enable change program implementation are identified and made in a timely fashion
- allocating the necessary resources to change program implementation and resolving any policy questions that may arise during implementation

The steering committee is intended to be a transitional body that will fade away once the change program has established a firm foundation and once the board's new standing committees are able to oversee implementation of change initiatives. For example, let us say that our hypothetical Metropolis Chamber of Commerce decided—in addition to establishing a new planning and business development committee—also design and implement a new planning process that would promote stronger board leadership in planning. The design and implementation of the improved planning process might validly be left to the new planning

WHEREAS, The HIDA Board of Directors, President and Executive Team are strongly committed to the proactive, creative management of change in the best interest of HIDA's members and health industry distributors generally; and

WHEREAS, The HIDA Board of Directors, President and invited guests conducted a strategic work session on June 14-16, 1994, as a key milestone in HIDA's strategic planning process; and

WHEREAS, The June 14-16 strategic work session focused on HIDA's values, vision, mission, and strategies, identified critical issues facing HIDA, and generated numerous ideas for strengthening HIDA's services to its members; and

WHEREAS, The consultant retained by HIDA to facilitate the June 14-16 strategic work session has submitted a set of detailed recommendations that are intended to ensure that HIDA realizes a full return on its investment of time and money in the June 14-16 strategic work session;

THEREFORE, BE IT RESOLVED THAT:

The HIDA Board of Directors generally accepts the consultant's report and recommendations and commits to timely action to ensure that the June 14-16 strategic work session yields a significant return to HIDA and to its members;

The HIDA Board of Directors hereby establishes the HIDA Strategic Development Program for the sole purpose of overseeing and directing implementation of the recommendations in the consultant's report;

And the HIDA Board of Directors hereby authorizes the HIDA Board Chair to appoint an Ad Hoc Strategic Development Program Steering Committee, which is to review the consultant's recommendations in detail, to tailor the recommendations to HIDA's unique needs, capabilities, and circumstances, to develop an implementation plan, and to oversee implementation, ensuring that the Board of Directors is consulted in a full and timely fashion on all implementation matters requiring Board attention.

Exhibit A. Resolution Text

and business development committee, working closely with the chamber chief executive. The change program steering committee would be accountable for launching the new planning and business development committee, but would not become involved in designing the new planning process.

Ensuring High-Level Staff Support

An association's change program cannot succeed without staff support. One approach that works is to assign an existing member of the association executive team to wear the "hat" of the change program coordinator in addition to his or her regular duties. The change program coordinator would be the hands-on executive responsible for day-to-day operation of the program, ensuring that it is on schedule and resolving operational issues as they arise. One of the preeminent responsibilities of the program coordinator would be to prepare the comprehensive action plan for steering committee review and adoption. In addition, the program manager would provide staff support to the steering committee:

- ensuring that steering committee meetings are scheduled as needed
- preparing agendas and other documentation for committee meetings
- monitoring program progress and briefing the committee regularly
- collecting information and performing analysis as needed for the committee
- documenting and following up on committee actions

Serving as program coordinator would not, of course, be a full-time responsibility, and it should be assigned as an additional duty to a member of the association's executive team. The responsibilities associated with the management of large-scale change are so complex and demanding, and the stakes involved for an association so high, that only an executive-level staff person should be assigned this role; it should never be considered merely a matter of administrative assistance.

The Ideal Coordinator

What kind of executive team member is likely to succeed in handling the program coordinator role in addition to his or her regular duties? The person should be:

- an ardent change champion, strongly committed to the planned changes
- highly skilled in, and passionate about, planning and project management. The role cannot be performed adequately by a "big-picture" type who has trouble getting down to details, or by a person who finds the management of process a bureaucratic irritant
- strong in written and oral presentation skills

- possessed of the kind of executive presence that commands respect and builds confidence and commitment
- highly compatible with the chief executive officer
- very flexible and a virtuoso at juggling complex demands without the threat of a nervous breakdown
- an earnest learner, open and questing in acquiring the skills required for successful change management

A True Partnership

The day-to-day relationship of the association chief executive and the program coordinator is critical to the coordinator's—and ultimately the program's—success. In the first place, access to the chief executive must be easy and frequent. Especially in the early days of the Program, there will be a number of questions that demand the chief executive's attention. If the program coordinator has trouble getting past the chief executive's secretary, his or her status will quickly decline in the eyes of peers and, of course, program implementation will be set back.

In a very real sense, the most successful program coordinator will become an alter ego to the chief executive, helping the chief executive to play the leading role in the change program and building a working partnership characterized by strong mutual trust and respect. If the two conflict to any significant degree in personality or style and are thus uncomfortable in each other's company, the partnership will be far less likely to work.

Comprehensive Action Plan

The comprehensive change program action plan is the major vehicle for setting the pace of change, ensuring that all of the steps involved in implementing targets are well-thought through and sequenced appropriately, and monitoring implementation as it moves forward. Developing the plan would be the first and foremost job of the program coordinator. The steering committee should set aside at least a half-day for reviewing and revising the plan.

Communicating With Members

One of the top priorities to be addressed in the plan is how to inform the membership, especially active volunteers, of the planned change initiatives that have resulted from the board-staff retreat. It is essential not only that the anticipated changes be understood, but also that they not be perceived as impugning current practices that may involve volunteers or in some way downgrading volunteer participation.

To take a practical example, let us take an association that has relied in the past on volunteer, nonboard participation in programmatic committees (such as a chamber's legislative affairs committee or an annual conference planning committee). If these committees have been viewed as an integral part of governance, then establishing new governance committees that will oversee, if not displace, the current programmatic committees can easily be seen as downgrading volunteer involvement. The comprehensive change program plan must address this concern proactively, ensuring that the changes are fully explained and that volunteers are reassured their contributions are in no way being diminished.

Complex Planning Challenge

Returning to the Metropolis Chamber of Commerce example, let's take one of the key initiatives in its change program—the establishment of four new governance standing committees to replace the existing programmatic committees. While this may seem at first blush to be a fairly straightforward change target, a number of complex, hard-to-implement steps must be addressed in the comprehensive action plan, including:

- drafting a bylaws revision, if necessary, and securing its adoption (Is a vote of the membership required? If so, when should it take place and how should the membership be briefed on the proposed revision?)
- fashioning a transition plan for phasing out the old committees and phasing in the new ones (with the very important goal of not derailing critical ongoing committee work or losing key initiatives through the proverbial cracks)
- developing a detailed charge for each of the new committees
- appointing committee chairs and members
- preparing and executing an orientation program for the new committees
- organizing the staff teams to support the committees and making sure they are well prepared to play their support roles
- planning the critical first meetings of the new committees

Missteps Can Be Costly

Any major misstep in the committee implementation process could damage the credibility of the change initiative and set back implementation. For example, the steering committee and program coordinator must make sure that the first meetings of the new standing committees are obviously well planned and executed. The new chairs must appear to understand the functions of the new committees inside-out and must handle their leadership roles capably, with no fumbling. The agendas of the kick-off meeting must also be substantive and interesting enough that attendees feel challenged and depart with a sense of satisfaction. It may make sense for this first meeting to focus on the development of a set of annual committee priorities and projected major accomplishments, and perhaps even a timetable.

Also of Help

The change program steering committee and program coordinator can take some relatively simple steps to facilitate Program implementation:

- Establish a central program headquarters—a kind of war room—perhaps by appropriating one of the association's conference rooms. The steering committee could hold its meetings here, and one of the walls might display a blown-up version of the comprehensive action plan.

- Provide board members and staff with three-ring binders for storage of all program-related information.

- Foster program identity by printing special letterhead stationery and perhaps even creating a simple logo.

- Disseminate regular bulletins that update all concerned on program progress.

- Have the chief executive and executive team set aside one meeting a month focusing on program implementation.

Chapter Fourteen
Sources of Inspiration and Information

Finding the Paths to Understanding

This concluding chapter is intended to be neither a comprehensive bibliography nor a detailed survey of pertinent literature. Rather, my intent is to suggest paths that the reader might take in search of information and inspiration for the board capability building journey. I would also like to share books and articles that have significantly influenced my thinking and consequently helped to shape this book.

The literature specifically focusing on nonprofit boards is not the only path worth traveling. Others areas that I have explored and found consistently useful are strategic planning and management, organizational innovation and change management, and human creativity and growth. I have cited only journals that have repeatedly proved their value to me and specific books and articles that I have read carefully more than once and whose ideas have had a significant impact on my work with nonprofit boards. I have also cited some of my own contributions to the literature that provide the reader with pertinent real-life cases. The curious reader will surely discover many other sources of inspiration and information in his or her own quest.

Association Management and *Leadership Magazine*, publications of the American Society of Association Executives, deserve special mention at the onset. They have over the years explored many of the issues dealt with in this book in articles of consistently high quality and relevance to practitioners. The reader should consider ASAE publications a reliable starting point for any of the paths to understanding.

Nonprofit Boards

Until relatively recently, the literature in the area of nonprofit board leadership has been scant, but the subject is receiving considerable attention these days and the body of published work is rapidly growing. Perhaps the best overall source of knowledge on the subject is the National Center for Nonprofit Boards. Headquartered in Washington, D.C., this organization promotes research and writing on nonprofit governance. Its very readable and practical monographs cover virtually every facet of nonprofit board leadership and development.

The reader should also keep in mind the importance of ASAE as a "first stop" for association board members and executives looking for practical wisdom on board leadership. *Leadership Magazine* is an especially rich resource in the governance field. The reader will find particularly interesting an *Association Management* article presenting a board leadership design case on which this book draws: Alan Beals' and Douglas C. Eadie's "Designing Board Governance" (August 1994, p. 129).

Of the academic journals, *Harvard Business Review* is without peer in publishing insightful pieces on governance aimed at board members and chief executives generally. In recent years, the *Review* has paid considerable attention to the nonprofit sector. For example, two recent articles on the subject that the reader will find useful are: William G. Bowen's "When a Business Leader Joins a Nonprofit Board" (September-October 1994, p. 38), and Regina Herzlinger's "Effective Oversight: A Guide for Nonprofit Directors" (July-August 1994, p. 52).

More practitioner-oriented and less concerned with theory is *Nonprofit World*, the journal of the Society for Nonprofit Organizations, headquartered in Madison, Wisconsin. *Nonprofit World* frequently publishes articles on nonprofit board leadership. In this regard, Eadie's and Richard L. Edwards' "Board Leadership by Design" (March-April, 1993, p. 12), discusses key elements of the design process, which are elaborated in Chapter 3.

A relative newcomer to the scene, *Nonprofit Management & Leadership*—published by Jossey-Bass and sponsored by the Mandel Center for Nonprofit Organizations at Case Western Reserve University, Cleveland—may over time become a valuable resource on board leadership.

Two books loom large in the field and are *must reading* on the journey. Cyril O. Houle's *Governing Boards* (Washington, D.C.: National Center for Nonprofit Boards, 1989) is a comprehensive primer that draws on extensive research and personal experience in covering every important aspect of nonprofit board operations. And John Carver's *Boards that Make a Difference* focuses on the policy formulation process as the preeminent board leadership tool, while also examining a number of related issues, such as board committees and the board-chief executive partnership.

Strategic Planning and Management

Hundreds of books and articles have been written on strategic planning and management over the past quarter-century, and hundreds more are on the way. The challenge is to sift through the abundant chaff in search of some wheat, avoiding the clear and present danger of being overwhelmed by the mechanics of planning. Since strategy is one of a nonprofit board's most important concerns, the search will be worth the effort to the reader.

The most useful book to date on nonprofit strategy is John Bryson's *Strategic Planning for Public and Nonprofit Organizations* (San Francisco: Jossey-Bass, 1989), which successfully balances a thorough description of up-to-date theory with numerous real-life examples. Professor Bryson, who is on the faculty of the Hubert H. Humphrey Institute of Public Affairs at the University of Minnesota, has produced a book that is refreshingly free of jargon and academic pretense, and its straightforward style makes for very pleasant reading.

One of the first books on public and nonprofit strategic management, John B. Olsen's and Eadie's *The Game Plan: Governance With Foresight* (Washington, D.C.: Council of State Planning and Policy Agencies, 1982) remains a reliable introduction to the subject.

Two monographs published by the National Center for Nonprofit Boards examine the role of the board in strategic planning and management. Dabney G. Park, Jr.'s *Strategic Planning and the Nonprofit Board* outlines the basic steps involved in the strategic planning process and discusses the role of the nonprofit board in the process. Eadie's more recent *Beyond Strategic Planning: How to Involve Nonprofit Boards in Growth and Change* describes how boards can have a significant impact on innovation and change by applying a contemporary version of strategic planning known as strategic issue management.

The *Harvard Business Review* has consistently published highly insightful, theoretically powerful articles on strategic planning and management with ideas that are applicable to the nonprofit association sector. One of the most influential in my work with nonprofit associations is Henry Mintzberg's "Crafting Strategy" (July-August 1987, p. 66), which provides an antidote to a tendency toward over reliance on formalism and rationality in strategic planning. In this beautifully conceived and written piece, Professor Mintzberg describes how strategic patterns often emerge over time and are eventually recognized, formalized, and adopted—rather than being consciously fashioned at the onset.

Two recent articles presenting in-depth strategic planning case studies on which this book draws are: Richard Jones' and Eadie's "Fostering Innovation and Growth" (*Nonprofit World*, January-February 1994, p. 23); and Evan Kemp's, Robert Funk's, and Eadie's "Change in Chewable Bites: Applying Strategic Management at EEOC" (*Public Administration Review*, March-April 1993, p. 129).

No serious student of the strategic planning process can ignore the fundamental contributions of Professor Nathan D. Grundstein, Emeritus Professor of Management Policy at the Weatherhead School of Case Western Reserve University. A penetrating critic of conventional wisdom who has little interest in the nuts and bolts of current planning practice, Professor Grundstein has produced three challenging books that explore the "foundations of the intelligence of strategic thinking." The reader will find most pertinent his third work, *The Knowledge of Strategy: Foundation for an Intelligence of Strategy* (Cleveland: Weatherhead School of Management, 1992).

Innovation and Change Management

A growing number of books and articles in the recent past have gone beyond the strategic planning framework in describing how organizations can successfully innovate and manage large-scale change. Three of the most powerful are Rosabeth Moss-Kanter's *When Giants Learn to Dance* (New York: Simon and Schuster, 1989); Peter M. Senge's *The Fifth Discipline* (New York: Doubleday, 1990); and Noel Tichy's *Managing Strategic Change*, (New York: John Wiley and Sons, 1983).

Also of interest to nonprofit board members and executives are Donald Kirkpatrick's *How to Manage Change Effectively* (San Francisco: Jossey-Bass, 1985) and Gareth Morgan's *Riding the Waves of Change* (San Francisco: Jossey-Bass, 1988). The reader will also find Glenn Tecker's and Marybeth Fidler's *Successful Association Leadership* (Washington, D.C.: ASAE Foundation, 1993) a useful survey of the skills need to manage change successfully in today's complex, rapidly changing environment.

A consistently valuable source on change management is the *Harvard Business Review*. For example, the November-December, 1993 issue features change management in four articles, which look at different facets of the process. The design role of the contemporary chief executive is explored in Robert Howard's fascinating piece, "The CEO as Organizational Architect: An Interview with Xerox's Paul Allaire" (September-October 1992, p. 106).

Human Creativity and Growth

Associations and their boards are above all else human beings. It stands to reason that the more these women and men are able to overcome limits to personal growth and to realize their full human potential, the more capable their organizations will be of successfully growing and managing change. Countless books and articles have appeared on this subject, and many more are on the way. To be sure, many are shallow, quick-fix-oriented, and gimmicky, but the discerning reader can find ample insight and inspiration.

A number of authors have explored the central place of principles and values in human growth. In this regard, Stephen R. Covey's *The Seven Habits of Highly Effective People* (New York: Simon and Schuster, 1989) is must reading, a virtuoso weaving together of psychology, spiritual values, strategy, and practical management techniques. Two highly popular books with a more spiritual bent that promote self-understanding and, hence, growth are Thomas Moore's *Care of the Soul* (New York: Harper Collins, 1992) and Scott Peck's *The Road Less Traveled* (New York: Simon and Schuster, 1978). As Dr. Peck makes so very clear, serious growth is not only a spiritual journey, it also requires tremendous discipline, courage, and tenacity. As the advertisement says, "No pain, no gain."

The reader will also find interesting Stratford Sherman's article, "Leaders Learn to Heed the Voice Within" in the August, 22, 1994 issue of *Fortune*. The piece introduces the current ideas, tools, and techniques available to those seeking greater self-knowledge.

Psychology and psychiatry are obviously a rich source on human growth. Rollo May's *The Courage to Create* (New York: W. W. Norton, 1994) vividly depicts the challenges to be expected in traveling the road of personal growth and presents the creative process as something very close to contemporary strategic management. Allen Wheelis' eloquent and elegant *How People Change* (New York: Harper and Row, 1973) is the most effective and moving descriptions of human growth through the path of psychoanalysis I have ever read. And the reader will also find useful James F. Masterson's *The Search for the Real Self* (New York: The Free Press, 1988), which sees the discovery of one's essential being as the preeminent key to a full, creative life.

And finally, Joseph Campbell explored in several works the power of myth in human understanding and growth, including his brilliant *The Hero With a Thousand Faces* (Princeton: Princeton University Press, 1949). The mythical hero's journey, says Campbell, is really an interior journey toward self-knowledge and the discovery of one's essential self—a journey fraught with peril and requiring a hero's daring. Professor Campbell became widely known through his filmed conversations with Bill Moyers, which were broadcast as a PBS series in the late 1980s. The transcript of these conversations was edited into a book well worth reading, *The Power of Myth* (Joseph Campbell with Bill Moyers, New York: Doubleday, 1988).

About the Author

Douglas C. Eadie is the founder and president of Strategic Development Consulting, Inc., a Cleveland, Ohio, firm specializing in nonprofit and public board development, strategic management system design and implementation, and executive team building. He has assisted over 200 nonprofit organizations around the country, including numerous associations. Prior to founding his firm, he held executive positions in several nonprofit and public organizations. He is the author of over 80 articles and book chapters and is coauthor of one of the first books on nonprofit and public strategic management, *The Game Plan: Governance With Foresight*. He is a Phi Beta Kappa graduate of the University of Illinois and earned his master of science in management degree from the Weatherhead School of Case Western Reserve University.